The Morning Of Your Wedding

Gretchen Maurer

authorHOUSE®

AuthorHouse™
1663 Liberty Drive, Suite 200
Bloomington, IN 47403
www.authorhouse.com
Phone: 1-800-839-8640

First published by AuthorHouse 6/11/2008

ISBN: 978-1-4343-3918-8 (sc)

Printed in the United States of America
Bloomington, Indiana

This book is printed on acid-free paper.

Contents

Chapter 3   70
The morning of: Your childhood home

Chapter 4   94
Unique Locations:

Chapter 5   **119**

Acknowledgements

Writing this book would not have been possible without my many wonderful brides! I loved being a part of so many wedding mornings! Thank you to Fritz, my husband for encouraging this project and being there for me in so many other ways. My two beautiful daughters, Kierstin and Amanda, bless you ladies for allowing me to enjoy my work and for modeling for me over the years. Thank you to my staff, Susan and Stacey for faithfully helping me, I miss you ladies! Also, thanks go out to Travis Flynn of Travis Flynn Photography who is a gifted artist, but also took the time to copy edit my book. Back cover photo credits belong to SM Cooper Photography.

Finally, my faith in Jesus has made life worth living, thank you God for beauty and blessings!

Introduction

Why an entire book dedicated to the *morning of* the wedding? Because every bride has one and *no one* has written about it!

Whether you are spending 5,000 or 500,000 dollars on your wedding you have to wake up somewhere, at some time and begin your day. How that infamous day starts is the key that will unlock the best possible route to your personal wedding fantasy, or worst nightmare.

Weddings are held just about anywhere today! But keep this in mind: no matter the location, every wedding *morning of* has its own set of challenges.

Why is there nothing written specifically about the wedding morning? Because no other vendor is present to experience all that happens. As an on-location hair and make-up professional, I am the *first* person the bride sees. Because of my experience at hundreds of wedding mornings at varied locations, I simply saw too *much* that should have been considered, better thought through or simply avoided altogether.

- **Wedding Bells Magazine notes: 61% of brides said they would have spent more time planning.**

As I researched to see what *has* been written about the *morning of*, I noticed that most books only dedicated a small paragraph that goes something like this:

Get your rest the night before. Eat a good breakfast and try to relax by getting a massage or taking a bubble bath.

So much for planning help! Something had to be done!

I saw:

- Too many brides who lost control or never had it.

- Family dynamics that could have been prevented.

- Hotel mornings completely unorganized.

- Lack of planning that created stressful home weddings.

- Morning food issues.

- Hangovers that hung on.

- Late attendants causing the photographer to play catch-up with the schedule.

- Unnecessary questions directed at the bride.

- Dogs who almost got the cake

- Cats that almost got the veil.

- Shutter-happy room crashers

- Pushy photographers

- Whiney children, crowded rooms, not enough showers, poorly packed bags and on and on.

Why am I qualified to be the one to write this book?

Here is *my* story. My husband and I are high school sweethearts. We got married in 1980. After one year of college, and as a 19year old newlywed, I went to hairdressing school and loved it. I immediately found my nitch in "dressing" hair. I loved styling special occasion hair. Even as a young stylist, I was given the brides.

In 1984 I took time off professionally to have my two daughters, one in '84 and one in '86. In 1989 my husband and I bought a salon in Orange, CT. In the early 90's I began teaching advanced updo classes and started to get my styles published. I appeared a few times on local TV and created a couple of teaching videos.

In 1994, burned out with the responsibilities of ownership and traveling, I closed the salon to work part-time so that I could be home more with my children. At this time I was approached to write the first ever bridal-based hair industry book, The Business of Bridal Beauty, published by Milady Publishing.

Salons have come a long way in catering to the bride, but at that time there was a lack of bridal skills and knowledge of the wedding industry.

- **When I taught my classes, many stylists acknowledged fear in dealing with the bride!**

Having taught stylists for 10 years about brides and weddings, a desire burned to bring what I knew about the salon industry to the wedding industry. Through The Association of Bridal Consultants (ABC), of which I became a member in 1996, I decided that a *"wedding"* per say between the two industries was necessary. Once involved, I spoke at many of their meetings and conventions, teaching the wedding planners how the salon industry worked.

Enter the boom of the internet! Another chapter was blooming for me.

When I had opened my salon in 1989, it was the first computerized salon in town. My dad had been a computer programmer since the 1960's, so I was indoctrinated early on. I watched as millions and millions of dollars were spent and lost as the Internet exploded into our homes. I decided to join in, and I bought the name weddinghair. com in 1998. Around the same time I injured my knee and needed surgery. Three screws in my knee later, I knew my days of standing behind the chair could not be forever. The Internet was the perfect venue to help thousands of brides at a time by sharing my bridal styles and tips.

I created Weddinghair.com, which offers a variety of updos and wedding hairstyles for every taste and every age. Each style is photographed in a step-by-step format with simple DIY directions. Some take the hair styling kits to their stylist, some try the design themselves and others bring them on their destination weddings.

- **Voted the #1 wedding beauty site by Brides magazine has been an honor.**

Now thoroughly indoctrinated in the wedding industry, the salon industry and the Internet, I felt there was still a piece of the pie missing!

This book you hold in your hands!

Allow me to share. Allow me to educate, so you can make some important decisions for your wedding morning ahead of time.

Below are some of the wedding morning locations at which I have performed beauty services, each with its own unique set of challenges:

- ❏ Salons
- ❏ Cramped hotel rooms
- ❏ Spacious hotel suites
- ❏ Tiny kitchens
- ❏ Huge kitchens
- ❏ Large dining rooms
- ❏ Bathrooms large enough to hold the ceremony
- ❏ Bathrooms that barely fit two
- ❏ Bedrooms of all sizes, shapes and décor
- ❏ Summer homes
- ❏ The mom's home
- ❏ The bride's home
- ❏ The bride and groom's home
- ❏ Banquet facilities
- ❏ Conference rooms
- ❏ Country clubs

❑ **Bed & Breakfasts**

❑ **Inns**

❑ **Grand mansions**

My prayer is that this book will empower you to experience your wedding day your way, with realistic expectations and great memories to recall for a lifetime.

God Bless and I hope I have helped!

Gretchen Maurer

Chapter 1

The Morning Of: Hotels & Resorts:

Many brides choose a resort location for their wedding ceremony and reception because most offer amenities that translate into mini vacations for their guests. This choice has both its perks as well as its own unique set of *morning of* challenges. One important suggestion I can offer is to try to visit your location the same time you will be having your wedding. The brochure will showcase picture perfect views of the ocean front bridal suite, but a wedding in mid July will be another ambiance altogether. The shore line may be dotted with colorful umbrellas and scantly clad guests may be wandering throughout the resort with tired kids in tow.

Hotels and Resorts offer one-stop shopping while providing services for the rehearsal dinner, the wedding ceremony and the reception. This makes the stress of wedding planning greatly reduced for all involved, especially if the wedding location serves as an in-between spot for both families and their guests. Many larger resorts and hotels even have their own in-house wedding planner which is fabulous!

- **What may seem more costly at first can very well be worth its weight in less stress and more fun!**

Guests and attendants can retreat to their rooms, and the children don't get under foot as much as they may at a home wedding. But even with all these pluses, don't leave all the planning to the hotel. In-house wedding planners are *in-house,* making sure their staff is on task. They don't usually become involved with the bride's personal morning needs. If you bring in your own planner, make sure everyone is on the same page and that your planner makes herself known early on.

Even with a planner you will still have many details of your *morning of* that you will need to give some thought, direction and attention.

Having spent a good part of my career on the call lists of vendor referrals, I serviced many brides who made their wedding dreams come true at these types of locations.

- **Make sure to check what their policies say about bringing in outside help.**

Having serviced weddings at *varied* locations, I have noticed that wedding guests behave in a more celebratory and party manner when at a larger hotel or resort. If this is your style then go for the big event! Also be aware that you will be sharing your day with complete strangers eager to catch a glimpse of the bride. With many of the guests also staying at the wedding location there is much more coming and going. Visiting and sightseeing may take up some of your *morning of* time. Initially this may seem like great fun to have everyone together, but gathering up a hotel full of relatives for the family pre-wedding portrait could prove to be a nightmare.

If you envision a smaller intimate event at a less marketed venue, this may require more research on your part, but it is well worth the effort for a perfect fit to your dream day.

Whether your choice is a wonderful resort or something chic and minimal, the key to a great *morning of* is reasonable expectations, organized planning and a balanced proper attitude.

Where will you sleep?

These may seem like dumb questions, but ask yourself what the answers to the following are:

- ❏ Are you getting ready at a hotel and sleeping there as well?

- ❏ Are you getting ready at one hotel and married off-site?

- ❏ Are you sleeping with your groom?

- ❏ Will you be kicking him out so you can get ready?

- ❏ Does he know where he is going?

- ❏ Is all of his stuff in one spot, or will he have to send back his best man for items he forgot in your room?

- ❏ Are you sleeping with your bridesmaids after a heavy night of dress rehearsal partying?

- ❏ Do you have your own room?

- ❏ Are you sleeping with your sister or maid of honor?

- ❏ Are you securing a suite?

❑ Is everyone getting dressed in your room?

❑ Does your mom, step mom, future mother in law/sister in law expect to be in on the dressing-together preparations?

❑ Who is helping grandma get dressed? Your mom? Where are they staying?

❑ Who is helping you?

❑ Who is helping the flower girl?

❑ Are you getting the same room for your first night as man and wife, or do you have to pack up and move all of your belongings to a new room?

These are all very important questions. As you read on, the answers will make all the difference.

Some brides choose to spend the night before with their fiancé. Because they live together anyways they feel it is no big deal. Saves a few bucks, right? But at what cost is peace!

As I arrived at one bride's hotel room, she was in the process of getting her groom out the door and he was not being too cooperative. They were fighting and she said, "Now I know why they say not to see each other the day of the wedding: it is too stressful!" Trust me, I did not write this book for nothing! The Wedding *morning of* is like no other! Plan on being separate the night before. It may make for a better start to the honeymoon!

Another bride and groom were moving their room to the bridal suit for their first night as husband and wife. Some wedding packages include this but packing to change rooms took up precious time from the *morning of.* They needed to be packed and out by a certain time yet needed items in their bags for the wedding morning. This can become very confusing and stressful.

Not all hotels are wedding-friendly:

Not all hotels are created equal when it comes to catering to a bridal party. For instance, economy hotels are simply not set up for the demands of a wedding party.

One young bride picked a small economy hotel to stay at the night before her wedding to balance out the cost of having her wedding at a local country club. Because of the time of her ceremony, the number of bridesmaids she had, and the travel time to the country club, my make-up artist and I told her we would need to arrive at 5:30am! Ouch! This is always an issue to consider when deciding what time to get married or how many friends to have in the wedding party. There were not a lot of happy bridesmaids that *morning of!* Trying to stay within a tight budget, she decided to share her room with three other women. When we were welcomed (sort of) into her tiny room, we could not even get past the door. It looked like a sorority party went on the night before! Clothes and suit cases had to be moved and a space cleared for our tools. Add to that, three additional bridesmaids from across the hall, one of whom brought her newborn baby with her that needed nursing; all came into the room to have their hair and make-up done! A congested bridal room is not conducive to a stress free *morning of!*

- **If you have to watch your budget, there are options to consider.**

Put your money where your best rest will be. Consider the following. Family and friends always ask what they can get for a wedding gift. You can't put a price tag on tranquility. Tell them it would mean so much to you if their gift would be to secure a large suite for your wedding party to get ready in. Maybe even an additional room adjoining, where one space can be for hair and make-up and the other room for getting dressed and the food spread.

- **If it is at all possible, sleep alone and get your rest!**

One bride had an adjoining living room area and galley kitchen for us to use to get the bridesmaids ready. Keep in mind these rooms are designed for two to four people at best. When you go for a tour of a proposed site, and blissfully wander through a suite, maybe taking an imaginary twirl in your perfect gown, STOP! Picture it full of people, because even three bridesmaids and a couple of moms will fill it up rather quickly, and don't forget to add in the stylists and photographer...and uncle Jack coming in to introduce you to his new wife, and your parents' best friends who knew you "way back when" and wanted to personally give you their gift because you "will be so busy later at the wedding" etc...etc...

Back to the bride; the floor plan was long and narrow with a fire place coming into the space and a coffee table between it and the sofa. My make-up artist had to use the mantel as a shelf for her make-up. I squeezed in at a table designed for four, turning one seat to the outside to do hair and fighting for table top space with water bottles, gifts and purses, hoping no one would be or become burned by the curling iron that is sure to topple over and maybe even melt a water bottle on the way!

- **If need be, move the furniture around or even remove it to accommodate the number of people.**

Ladies, as you visit locations to consider for your wedding morning, think of your wedding party and the number of people who will be joining you! Maybe this is the time to decide on keeping it smaller than you planned. However, this poor bride also committed the night before the wedding faux-pa; she had not gotten much sleep because she partied too hard and was hung-over! With her stomach unsettled and everyone asking questions she became a little overwhelmed. All of the bodies created more heat than the air conditioner could comfortably handle, so it was cranked to cold. A few of her friends who were smokers, stepped outside to do so, but the cigarette smoke made its way through the air conditioning ducts and back into the room. This added more pain to her hangover and more negative emotions to the atmosphere.

- **Also make note of this fact! Many air conditioning units are linked to the opening and closing of balcony or terrace sliding doors. If the door is left open even the slightest, the AC unit shuts off automatically. All of a sudden everyone is sweltering and can't figure out why.**

Her flower girl was not in the best of sorts either. Summer is high season for young tots to get viruses. When she should have been getting ready, her mom wanted her to nap so she would be in better spirits. As a mother, I agree; a nap outweighs cute curls any day. Be prepared to go with the flow!

On top of all this the bride had promised an old high school friend that she could hang out in the prep room, and she was not even in the wedding party! She was on a personal mission to create a candid scrapbook and kept taking pictures all morning! UGH!!

If you need your sleep and wish to be alone, be prepared to say so. Try not to let your younger sister or best friend talk you into a slumber party on your last night! Kick out your groom and if you don't feel like garnering up the patience needed to handle your mother-in-law, or your own mother for that matter, *gently* tell them it would be best if they got ready in their own rooms. Bottom line is you need your *sleep* and you need your *space*.

- **Make sure the location you choose for your wedding morning is wedding-friendly!**

Still want everyone there? Go for it! Just get enough space, be prepared for a bit of chaos and have a blast!

Time line interruptions:

Just because the resort may call one of their sleeping rooms the "bridal room" it may not work out for your *morning of* needs. Sometimes "this room" comes as part of a package, but you don't have to be stuck using it. If this room is too small, your morning time line can be jeopardized.

I frequently serviced many bridal parties at one resort where this "bridal room" was relativity small. The wedding parties that were a total of two to three people, were lovely and relaxing. Larger wedding parties in this "bridal room," simply became too stressful. Consider your *morning of* needs carefully. If your wedding party is staying at the same location and you hope for a quiet *morning of,* encourage (ask) them to get dressed in their own rooms or designate one of *their* rooms for dressing.

If you and your immediate family have rooms, but the bridal party members travel in that morning from other locations, then they will expect to be able to dress with you. Because of their gowns and toiletries, they will need more bathroom and dressing space. I have seen this happen a number of times and no one had thought to plan for it. Family members who were staying at the hotel were asked on the spot if bridesmaids could dress in their rooms. This does not go over well as the men don't like their ball games to be interrupted and the women feel they have to scrambled back to pick up the room.

- **There always seems to be someone who is concerned with modesty and locks herself in the bathroom to dress.**

Even if you secure a large suite with two bathrooms, depending on the size of your wedding party, things can still get tight and throw off your time line if you don't limit visitors, spouses and friends.

Another bride secured a lovely large suite. In addition to the large common area, it had two bed rooms, a full-size dining table, a bar that held the food spread and three bathrooms. The additional bathrooms were not comfortable for non-family to use because it meant they had to meander through someone's sleeping quarters. There was one bathroom in the common space that had a long mirror and sink at the end while a small separate room held a toilet and Jacuzzi tub.

- **This bride had envisioned a lovely relaxing morning to include a bubble bath in that tub.**

I am not kidding when I say the room was buzzing! Two men, one a brother-in-law and one a cousin, an elderly grandmother, the mother of the bride, the bride, five or six bridesmaids, a junior bridesmaid and one flower girl, plus myself and two additional stylists of my staff completed the body count in that small suite! The only downer of the morning was when the grandmother announced her diamond earrings were missing! I got sick to my stomach thinking about all the people who were in the room and that anything could have happened. This drove everyone off track for a time and thankfully she had simply forgotten where she had put them after the rehearsal dinner the night before. When I wasn't looking, a flower girl took some hair extensions off the table and wrapped them around her waist like a hula skirt!

As we continued to work on the others in the bridal party, the bride decided to put on a facial mask and "relax" in the Jacuzzi! Mind you, just on the other side of a piece of sheet rock was all this commotion. Then, one by one, everyone, *I mean everyone*, poked in their head to laugh at her and some even took pictures! It was a hoot! Thankfully the bride was goodhearted and took it in stride! Even her brother-in-law came out and said, "My chest is bigger than hers!" But all this excitement did not phase the bride one bit. Where the bride's attitude goes everyone follows!

- **Despite the commotion, in order to remain on or close to your time line, keep your eyes on the clock, because others can get carried away and take you with them!**

Sometimes the opposite of a full room happens and the bride is suddenly left alone with no one to help her manage the dress. Often with resort weddings people are spread out between rooms, buildings and timeshare condos on the property. Make sure whoever is to be at the *morning of* room to get dressed or have hair and make-up done has a schedule. Also try to obtain their room numbers, as not everyone reads their itinerary and they may need a call! Sometimes the hotel's location does not allow cell phones to work well, so it is hard to reach people to keep things on time. I will be in the room and someone will ask "Well where is (so and so)? Call her." They try, but many times they just don't have a signal.

Friends and guests can sometimes be down right oblivious about a wedding schedule and wander in saying, "Well I tried to get here on time, but Danny was not done with his omelet". Or a bridesmaid says, "The room was too crowded so I decided to get dressed in my own room". Meanwhile you had planned on passing out their gifts of matching necklaces, and you see she is already wearing something else, and you hate it!

At another resort wedding the bride was in the shower when I arrived. She was supposed to be ready for me with dry hair because I was going to use hot rollers which need the hair to be dry. Your stylist may suggest time saving tips that may not seem important to you. Blow-drying adds an additional half hour or more to the preparation time line per person! Multiply this by how many bridesmaids, who ignore directions and show up with wet hair, it could spell "time line out the window" disaster! Not only was this bride not as ready as she could have been, she had teenage children who kept coming into the room asking questions and complaining about what they had to wear. Some level of stress will simply be unavoidable. Control what you can, like getting into the shower on time.

- **Sometimes not even the bride realizes the morning should run on time.**

By the time her photographer came, she was not ready and this caused her to lose out on some key family photo opportunities. Many brides pay for a package to include specific photos, or they pay by-the-hour, but don't end up having time for all the shots they envisioned if they have a late start to their day.

- **Weddings are huge events that demand a timeline and a schedule no matter what their size or location.**

To keep the wedding *morning of* on track, have someone utilize the wedding rehearsal to remind everyone of the morning time line. If you have a wedding planner, ask her to make this announcement. Your mom or maid of honor can also fulfill this role. The *morning of* time line is just as important for a smooth start to your day. It does not hurt that the men also sit through this speech. Remember, if you fail to plan, plan on failing.

Beauty services and options to consider:

If you have it within your budget to bring in your own hair and make-up artist, there are a number of things to consider. Experience in doing weddings is key! Many photographers can offer up their own horror stories of blaming the hair and make-up artists for causing the wedding to run late! Because everyone is anxious about getting dressed up and looking perfect, selecting a professional and experienced team of stylists is a must!

1. **First, how many stylists do you need for the size of your wedding party and family members?** Consider that family members may also need services especially if they have traveled in for your wedding. They may assume they can piggyback on your stylists and this is not fair to the stylist or good for the time line. Having a head count will help the stylist remain on or close to schedule and allow them to figure out an approximate start time.

2. **Sometimes the mother or mother of the groom and her daughters will insist on bringing in their own stylist.** At first you may be annoyed or feel like they are being controlling, but this can be great. It saves you time and stress and they get exactly what they want. Just be sure to gather all the details ahead of time. If your team of stylists quoted you on 13 people and now they have only 8 to do, they will still charge for 13.

3. **Others insist on going to their own stylist or doing their own hair because they don't trust anyone else, and you were hoping for a cohesive look.** As they come back with their perfect blowout, they see everyone else is getting an updo and now want *your* stylist to do "something special" with them. *Yup it happened, more times than I can remember.*

4. **This may also happen with the make-up**. One wedding stands out in particular. My make-up artist did a lovely job with the entire wedding party, however the groom's sister insisted on doing her own make-up. Her make-up "look" was more appropriate for a night of clubbing so it certainly did not look suitable for this morning wedding!

5. **A bridesmaid cannot afford to pay for her services.** She may not tell you this is the reason she is declining services. To prevent plain Jane from getting lost in the photos, offer to pay for her make-up. Here is another out-of-the box thought. Your gift to your bridesmaids could be paying for their beauty services. Or you can cover the cost for one or two who do not have the extra cash. When finalizing our *morning of* plans at the trial run some brides have asked me ahead of time to include so and so in the services. I get to whisper in her ear that the fee has been taken care of and offer her a turn. It is always wonderful to do this for someone.

One poor bride was all over the hotel trying to gather her guests for their *morning of* services. She had secured a conference room to do hair and make-up. I think every female was invited for services (or it seemed so) that morning! Everyone was traveling in from out-of-state and this was a wonderful gesture. Normally, when hair is done in a guest room, women wander in and out in all stages of dress, robes and the like. But since everyone had to shower and dress and *then* find their way to the conference room it took up some precious time. This did not stop the bride's mother: she simply wandered around the hotel in her short silk robe mortifying the poor bride!

A number of teens were also receiving services that morning. Teens tend to shower right before they have to get ready, and with their thick healthy hair it simply takes more time than others. People tend to assume that stylists will do wedding day hair like they do it themselves, so many figure it needs to be freshly washed. This is not the case in "dressing" hair or doing an updo. For most bridal styles it is best to shampoo the evening before. If there are a number of teens and Jr. Bridesmaids who need to get ready, it may help to let their mother know if the stylist requests they show up with dry hair. A good wedding stylist will know the importance of a wedding morning time line, and give directions accordingly. As the bride, you need to communicate this to your party ahead of time.

Many times a family member will offer to provide hair services for everyone the *morning of.* If you know them well and love their work, then go for it. If they are also in the wedding party, it may just add to their stress. I had one bride who felt obligated to allow her aunt to do her wedding hair. To keep the morning as simple as possible she had her aunt do *just* her hair and she hired my team to do all the rest of the 9 or so bridesmaids!

- **A family member or friend may do a great job, but the pressures of a wedding morning of may affect their work and your relationship.**

Ask them if they have done weddings and insist on a trial run even if they say it is not necessary. One hairdresser friend shared that as an invited guest, she was also going to do everyone's hair at the wedding. But her luggage never showed up with all of her tools and pins! A frantic trip to the local drug store for pins and spray caused a lot of undue stress. Keep this in mind.

Hire a professional wedding hair specialist if you can as opposed to the hotels spa and beauty staff unless you have some good references. The atmosphere of a spa is not conducive to the atmosphere of a bustling wedding party! A wedding specialist will have their own system, the hotel spa may not. Not all stylists are created equal. Not every stylist can do or enjoys doing all services. Some love color, some love cutting, but only a few love brides. In any given salon or spa environment, there may be only one or two who service brides.

- **These days bridal hair is a specialty requiring someone who is well versed in styling bridal hair and the workings of a wedding morning of timeline.**

This may mean your favorite stylist is not one of them, forcing you to look elsewhere. The pressures of an entire wedding party plus unfamiliar surroundings, such as a hotel desk chair or no mirror to work behind, may shake the confidence of your favorite stylist requiring you to consider the hotels staff. If you loved the way your stylist did your hair for the prom but she is trying to tell you she does not like to do wedding parties, don't pressure her. During your interview process make sure you are completely comfortable with the design, professionalism and personality of the hotel staff.

If you choose this route, make sure you plan on having a trial run when you visit the location, preferably with the same person who will do your hair on your wedding morning!

The hotel's wedding services may include the additional choice of a spa package or a massage. Before purchasing a spa package consider the time line of your morning. If services will be squeezed into a couple of hours, then ask if you can skip the massage, because it will be anything other than relaxing. I remember one bride running in late for her hair and make-up after receiving her massage. She said it was too hard to relax, and she felt her hair getting greasy and knew she did not have time for a second shower and shampoo! Ask if this dollar amount can be substituted for something else more enjoyable like a round of mimosas and a bowl of fresh strawberries for the wedding party.

If you *are* massage savvy and this is a must have for your *morning of*, then consider the time of your ceremony and number of attendants to make this treat possible for yourself.

- **Some resorts have an in-house make-up artist but no hair stylist.**

Make-up artists are a lot easier to find than wedding hair specialists. I prefer to work with my own make-up artist because we work simultaneously which is a time saver, but there have been many occasions when I had to work with others. At one hotel wedding I was doing only hair in the bride's suite. Outside help was not welcome in the hotels spa/salon. The hotel make-up artist, who did not come up to the room, insisted that everyone have their hair completely finished before she would do any make-up. This was revealed only after I sent a bridesmaid down for her make-up while in hot rollers and she was sent back upstairs announcing she was refused services. Then we double stepped it to finish everyone's hair and sent them down for make-up. This way of receiving services takes up more time. It would have been helpful if the hotel told the bride this up front. I did not even think to ask, so I am mentioning it here!

One bride who hired my hair services decided to save money by not using my make-up artist and hired someone from a mall make-up counter. Now by no means am I saying there is anything wrong with this, there are fabulous make-up artists at the mall counters. My make-up artist started her career at the mall counter.

- **The make-up artist's talent was not the issue with this particular wedding; professionalism and communication were.**

Instead of driving to the resort as the make-up artist said she would, she changed her mind and took a train instead, and then a cab. Plus, she did not tell the bride of the changes and she did not have a cell phone. This ran her almost two hours behind and the bride grew frantic by the minute, making it hard for me to do my work! *You* may know how long the drive will be to the hotel, but inexperienced vendors may simply be naive concerning wedding protocol, change their minds and not think anything of it.

- **Though they may be fabulous artists, make sure to find out how much experience they have traveling on location and get references.**

Once she finally did get started, she worked slowly and the bride kept telling her how much time she had left, and of course everything ran behind. The humorous side to this story is, the bride was a wedding planner! Remember, mall makeup artists are sales people, trained to work in detail, slowly enough to hook you and make their quota. This young lady simply did not have enough experience to step it up for a wedding. The wedding morning needs to be in another gear, not rushed, but with a flow and an atmosphere of calm and confidence. Service, not sales is a free lance artist's goal.

Off location beauty services:

If your hotel or resort wedding location requires you to travel far from home, you may not have it in your budget to bring your own stylist. If the hotel does not offer in-house services, then an area salon may be the answer. The hotel may have a list of suggestions or you can let your fingers do the clicking online. Traveling off site to a salon will depend greatly on the time and day of your wedding, as well as how many will need services. A Friday night wedding is the easiest to accommodate as you have a good part of the day free. When searching online I suggest you look at the best salons that have a beautiful web site and some type of bridal advertising. Top salons require more stringent hiring of talent, though a great wedding stylist at a small town salon is a hidden treasure; if you can find him or her.

For those who will be going to a salon, make sure to leave enough time for services and travel. If your trial run is in March and your wedding is in July, make sure to ask the stylist how the traffic is in the summer, and give yourself extra time if need be.

Look on my web site, Weddinghair.com, as I have national listings of hundreds of salons. I don't personally know them or even their skill level, but they asked to be posted so that says they want to service brides! Also, call more than one hotel in your area for referrals.

If you need early Saturday services or Sunday services, it may take a bit more searching to find an off location salon, so get on top of your beauty needs as soon as you have your location secured.

- **Not all salons will send out their stylists to come on location.**

Some feel weddings are not cost effective. For the time it takes for an average stylist to do an updo, they can do two or three haircuts and make more money. For those salons that *will* send out stylists, be prepared to spend double or triple in salon fees to make up for this difference.

I have had a few resort weddings where the bride was coming from across the country and had no way of getting a trial run. If you absolutely have no way to receive a trial run, the stylist should be willing to communicate with you thoroughly. I make sure to exchange photos online and talk a number of times to get everything just right. One bride decided to get a trial run locally and then brought me the photos. This helped her feel safe, and it was a great help seeing what she wanted.

- **I strongly suggest using e-mail for all corresponding, and these should be kept and referred to as the wedding gets closer.**

A stylist may be excellent at hair but not too good at the business end, as mentioned earlier. *You* will need to be if she is not, for your own peace of mind.

When booking my wedding clients, I filed my brides by their wedding date first and their name second. There were times when I had a couple of brides with the same first name. I would always ask for her wedding date as well so I knew who I was talking to.

- **Don't be offended when any vendor does not remember you right away.**

But if they can't pull your paper work quickly and this occurs every time you call don't ignore these red flags. An organized vendor is equally important as a talented one.

Into the dress and morning emotions:

There comes a moment in the morning when the spirit in the air changes. It happens for every bride and every wedding. And it happens just before putting on the gown. No matter what is done or left undone, once the gown is on, it is like stepping onto one of those moving floors at the airport. She is out of the gate and the day is on auto pilot.

- **Some brides are determined not to be nervous.**

Friends will pop in and ask "How are you doing, are you nervous?" and she will reply, "No, not really. I thought I would be." But eventually even the stealthiest bride begins to get nervous. Nervous means a lot of different things for different people. Some brides get quiet and have a hard time making a simple decision. Others can't eat. There are those who become chatter boxes while some turn into control freaks asking where everyone is, "Are they getting ready?" and "Where are my flowers!"

One of my very easy brides was sweet and calm all morning. I was in her room doing her hair, her mom's and her grandmother's. My make-up artist and another stylist were in another room doing everyone else. This bride's mother-in-law was a seamstress and was from Italy, with a thick accent. She was hand stitching the bride's gown! Right there and then that morning! In her European way, she insisted on making it perfect! I could tell the bride was stuck between a rock and a hard place; she was not too happy this was happening. She had attempted to say her gown was fine and for her mother-in-law not to fuss but it came to no avail. Well the bride was finally ready to put on the dress, which was very simple in a soft flowing fabric with a small train. Her mother stood behind her zipping her up. The bride took one step and RIP! Her mother had been standing on the train! Though there were sounds of damage, nothing showed and the bride was not about to get out of that dress! This sweet bride became firm and determined to get out of that room!

This poor mother of the bride! Not only did she feel the tension the mother-in-law brought to the room, she stepped on her daughter's gown and she also had to get her elderly mother dressed. Many times mothers and grandmothers are not accustomed to getting so dressed up. They may go through months of dieting, perhaps some plastic surgery, suffocating girdles, heals or tight shoes making them irritable and nervous themselves. Sometimes mom is not much help to her daughter!

Sometimes the daughter does not *want* her mothers help. There is nothing wrong with this, but try to have a plan or conversation well in advance as to how the morning dressing is going to unfold to keep emotions in check. You may adore your mom, but you know her presence would be too stressful. Here are a few of the mom scenarios I have seen unfold at hotel and resort weddings:

- I have seen some well intentioned daughters try hard to allow their mom in the room, but you could cut the tension with a knife.

- I have seen an aunt or a sister taking a silent clue from the bride to get the mom out of the room.

- I have been told ahead of time the mom was asked not to come.

- And I have seen a few manipulative mothers show up anyways.

- One bride didn't care how it made her look. She was so angered by her mothers' intrusion and asked, "Why are you here? I asked you not to come." This made it very uncomfortable for everyone.

- I have seen many lovely mornings unfold with mom included, knowing her place while allowing the bride to have her moment.

- Discuss ahead of time who will help the bride get into the dress; don't assume it will be the maid of honor or the mother.

I have seen too many mothers trying to get their husband ready, and a grand kid or two plus their own mother. They were no help to the bride. I have seen maids of honor who were simply clueless or so stressed that they were little help to the bride.

Another one of my brides had a sister who was her maid of honor. But this sister was also in charge of getting their mother who was in a wheel chair to the wedding, plus she had a husband and two small children! She went back and forth between the three rooms all morning!

Pick your calmest friend to help you dress! One hotel bride asked a dear friend who was not a bridesmaid to help her dress. This was a great idea! She felt needed; she was not stressed trying to get herself ready, and it really worked well!

Nail down as many details as you can in order to prevent crowded rooms, mother-in-law issues and ripped trains!

Packing:

Make a list and check it twice! Here is something we can learn from the jolly old guy in the red suit who made this statement so famous. Now, he makes this run around the world every year so you'd imagine he has it all figured out, right? But he still uses a list! Well, a wedding is a one-time affair and you have one chance to get it somewhat right. All those planning books are on the shelves for a reason. The authors are trying to help you get things under control, reduce the stress and banish fears. This is what I think of a list.

- **A list is not something I need because I'm forgetful or stupid, it is my brain on paper and once it is on paper, I don't have to keep it in my head any longer than it needs to be.**

The mind is free to think of other things. Next, a list should get transferred to a calendar so items can be tackled or delegated one at a time and on time.

In the prime of my career when I had two young kids at home, my business to run and was on the road doing hair shows, I *even* wrote down when I would *think* about something. I remember my brother calling me to ask about an upcoming event and I told him I was not thinking about "that" until the following week and I would get back to him then!

I believe the unavoidable stress associated with wedding planning can be lessened greatly with education, common sense, balanced expectations and lists! Having a list will help you with packing and prevent unnecessary stressful moments.

Getting dressed at a hotel or resort requires more packing and travel than getting ready at home. You have to pack up all your toiletries, everything that will go on your body and what you will be taking for your honeymoon. You don't want to forget your jewelry or perfume or your headpiece! This alone is difficult if you recall the stress with getting ready for a trip. Now add in a wedding ceremony, relatives and the like!

Make a list! And this is not just a one-time deal.

- **Keep a pad near you at all times, especially toward the end of your planning, as things will come to you all hours of the day and evening!**

One poor bride of mine wasted close to an hour looking for her tiara, which she thought she had lost off the luggage cart on the way up to her hotel room. She had the entire hotel looking for it! She thought it was in a certain plastic bag but it was not. I can't tell you how many times she opened up that pink bag and said, "I know I put it in here. It must have fallen out". I kept asking her if everything was out of the car, and eventually she had someone go back to the car and look. There it was in the back seat. She forgot that she had moved it to a different bag! Whew! This type of *morning of* stress usually lands in my lap to fix as I have to clam down the bride so she can focus on getting ready. Now I must work *fast* to make up for the lost hour yet not *look* like I am.

Designate a packing area. Don't be a procrastinator! Your life is basically on hold as wedding plans take over, so go with the flow!

- **Designate one room, "zone" or area, wedding-packing-central.**

As your items are purchased, put them on the table: make-up, perfume, hose, shoes, lingerie, jewelry, tiara etc. I am also a firm believer of keeping things off the floor to reduce stress and clutter. Don't try to take a bunch of small random bags with you to your wedding morning. You will forget what is inside and because they can be slippery they may be easily lost. If you must use a bag, a roll of masking tape is great for writing down the contents. Stick it where you can read it, prior to packing the items inside in a more suitable traveling container.

- **Don't put anything on the floor of a closet!**

As you near your date and you stop wearing the clothes you want to take on your honeymoon, put them out so you can see what you have and what still needs to be purchased, washed or made ready for packing.

As you pack, go over your checklist. Make one list for the wedding day and one for the honeymoon. Keep your wedding *morning of* items together. This organization will also help when you send your relatives home with the items you are not taking to the honeymoon.

Food for the morning:

Ahh! The comfort of food! What better way than to have something wonderful to eat as you and your friends are getting ready for the wedding day. Food evokes memories, calms nerves, and adds to the social environment. At a number of wedding mornings I have attended, food was not planned out ahead of time or it was not thought of at all.

- Some brides do not have a mother or older woman in attendance to think of these things.

- Some brides don't eat in the morning themselves, so they don't think of it for others.

- Some brides pack their own snacks, but chips and pretzels are not enough to hold everyone until the reception.

- Some brides eat with their families in the morning, but others coming may not have eaten, assuming they would be fed.

Many times the bridal party misses out on the cocktail reception because they are off taking pictures. You don't want anyone to be miserable for the pictures or pass out from lack of food!

Remember the frat party bride? Aside from there hardly being any room for beauty services and none for dressing, the food situation was not planned for either. Some small hotels may not even have room service, and this was one of them. Someone brought a box of Munchkins, but this was hardly enough. One maid went downstairs to the continental setup, brought up a bowl of cereal and tried to eat it balancing on the bed. Others, in rollers, were not brave enough to venture out. Then the bride's dad popped in with his girlfriend and they were swiftly enlisted to take a coffee and bagel sandwich order. But he had no idea where to go, and by the look on his face this was not something on *his* to-do list that morning! Luckily my make-up artist and I were local and knew where to send him, but this did not stop the infamous takeout mishaps from occurring! If a bride does not get her coffee the way she likes it, watch out! I have seen my share of whining brides crying over their toast and coffee disappointments.

- **Never have I seen a takeout order come back 100% correctly at any wedding morning of I have serviced!**

It is best if a box of Joe is purchased and a variety of bagels and donuts are put out so the wedding party can all make their own choices from there. I know this sounds silly, but make sure the food is taken out of the bags and put on plates. I have seen bags of food sit there because people hate to be seen going into the bag. It "feels" impolite for some to do this. Not every bridesmaid knows everyone and if the food is accessible it will get eaten.

If a continental breakfast bar is available, send someone down to ask for a tray so a sampling of foods can be brought up for everyone who is a hotel guest. This can also be discussed when booking your room.

As a gift to you, someone may enjoy covering the cost of catering a lovely fruit and bagel tray to be brought up to your room. It may not be able to be delivered straight from the café, as many hotels don't allow food to be ordered off the premises. But as a gift basket or gift tray it could be brought in by a friend or relative.

At one resort wedding, friends of the bride's parents came up to visit the *morning of* room and saw the fun everyone was having but realized it was not their place to stay. So in order to be a part of the fun without getting in the way, they decided to send up champagne for all to enjoy! The bride was very pleasantly surprised.

- **Some brides provide lovely snack baskets for everyone.**

If preparation time for hair and make-up is planned remotely near a mealtime, plan ahead for some kind of food to be brought in. If the formal wedding food is hours away, it is best if some type of fruit and cheese spread is put out. Protein is a good choice. Also bottles of water, coffee and juice should be provided. I have seen maids running around the hotel looking for dollar bills and a soda or snack machine when they should be getting their hair set! Especially if there are children involved, provide food.

When food is not planned, someone always decides they are hungry and looks over the room service menu. The morning usually goes as follows: they talk about what to order for at least 15 or 20 minutes, figuring out who wants what, who will share with whom, who's going to pay, who has cash, who's going to put it on their card, is there an ATM in the lobby, who's boyfriend has their purse etc…) The call is made and they wait and wait. The food finally arrives and they have to take bites between hairspray and lip-gloss! Or they barely have time to even eat!

One bride got married near Halloween and someone brought in candy. Everyone munched down peanut butter cups! Not the best choice for nerves!

Sometimes the bride has decided to take *all* of the wedding party photos *before* the wedding and then the family photos later. This calls for an early start as well and the need for a meal.

Depending on the time of the ceremony and the size of the party, sometimes two meals need to be provided for everyone. My staff and I serviced a very large wedding party out-of-state, and they had to put us up the night before. Twelve people were to be serviced starting at 6 am. Both breakfast and lunch were in order, as the wedding was an evening affair. We arrived to a large suite strewn with cots and sleeping maids!

- **The bride's family wanted the exclusive address for the wedding, but they saved money on room costs by squeezing in cots.**

Bagels, fruit and coffee were ordered *after* the mother tried to ask who wanted what. The spread was lovely, but it was ordered too late. If you know for sure you will be doing this, do not wait until everyone is hungry! With fifteen people starting their day so early, don't waste time to see what people want; just order! For some reason the lunch *was* planned ahead.   But by the time the morning   food came and the girls got ready, the lunch tray from a local sandwich shop arrived shortly thereafter.

- **Not one person had any of the food that was planned for lunch.**

Someone had order a grinder tray and there it stood, plastic wrap on and untouched, while the girls milled around too dressed up to deal with grinders and too full from the late breakfast. Boy, would I have loved one of those sandwiches as we had been working non stop for hours! But there were so many girls in the room and by now it was a maze of gowns in the way. My staff and I could not even get close to the table and it was not even offered!

- **Please consider feeding the stylists if it is hours of work.**

Some brides are so gracious and order enough for us to eat while others neglect us all together. In the morning I always arrive fed and ready to work, but a few hours in and it is nice to be offered something more to eat.

One wedding party had secured a time-share condo on the resort's property. These can be great because they have a small kitchen. But this wedding party did not plan ahead. They just had soda and water in the room. It was an evening wedding and the maids became hungry. They decided on room service, but because the food and kitchen were located in the hotel a few buildings away; it took forever to arrive. Many resorts host two or more weddings at a time. If it is vacation season, room service may be nearly impossible to reach for services. I have even seen the phone go unanswered numerous times!

When it comes to food for the wedding party, here are some creative options:

- Do a search online for a local coffee/pastry shop you can order from.

- Pre-order a tray of goodies ahead of time or have them delivered, if possible.

- Put someone who is not in the wedding party in charge of the food.

- Is there a guest or family member who lives near the wedding location? They may enjoy putting out a spread of goodies to bring up to your room.

- Delegate one of the groomsmen to pick up preordered food. This is a great job for a guy; hey, it's food!

One groomsman was husband of the year. He simply showed up with a big box of coffee, bagels and muffins. It was the best. Everyone just dug in.

For lunch, a tray of wraps makes for a great feast. Remember, usually there are no tables to sit at, so simple finger food works best. Tabletop space may become limited as hair and make-up items are spread out, the flowers arrive and purses and gifts multiply. I have seen maids order a salad and try to eat, balancing it on their lap or sitting on the floor with their legs under a small coffee table! For a light lunch, another great idea is to have someone pack a picnic basket with cheeses, pretzels, trail mix, crackers, small chocolate bars, wines, bottle waters, juices and fresh fruits. Grazing and munching is always welcome. People pop in to visit and chat, so there is not really any time for sit-down eating. If the wedding is an evening affair, plan a brunch just before services are to begin, making sure it does not linger into the hair and make-up time slot. Do provide drinks all day and something for the stylists to eat.

Siblings-teens-children and the emotions which follow:

Remember the frat party bride, again? Crowded room, no food, messed up coffee order, nursing bridesmaid and to top it off the bride's younger sister had herself a complete melt down! Unfortunately it started with her hair. She was tired of getting the same old barrel curl updo she had for all of her school dances and wanted something different. (Weddings are never a good time to try something *different*.) Her *different* hair style *was* beautiful and just like the picture she had picked out, but a deeper issue became the trigger of her uncertainty. After we clamed her down and got the hairdo drama settled, (back to her old stand-by-style) she was able to verbalize that it was in fact *not* the hair style but her fear of losing her best friend, her big sister. My make-up artist was a pro at comforting anyone who was upset (love you Susan) and was able to uncork the true feelings behind the waterworks. Her make-up had to be reapplied and so did the bride's, because once she learned of her sister's real fears and had a sister heart-to-heart, the bride was crying too!

- **Hire trained professionals as we have experience in all wedding morning of related issues.**

One beautiful bride was getting married without the blessing of her parents and against their wishes. They were not even coming to the wedding. The only one of the bride's 10 siblings who came was her younger sister. However the groom had a sister, and she and their mother wanted to come to the room in the morning to be a part of the getting-ready festivities. Well this bride was not in the best of moods considering the snubbing of her family and could not understand why her mother-in-law and her sister-in-law wanted to be there. The bride called down to the front desk and told them not to give out her room number as she did not want anyone to come in!

Second weddings usually include children and can come with their own unique set of *morning of* issues and emotions. Because a hotel or resort wedding is more public, the children and teens try to get away with more. Sometimes the children resent the new groom and are not too cooperative about behaving during the *morning of* preparations. Sometimes one child does great while the other one acts out. Don't try to *make* anything "happen". Feelings run deep and at their young age they simply cannot understand everything. Let it go. It takes the steam out of their sails if they see they can't get you upset.

Young bridesmaids are more common with second weddings as children and step children are coming together to create a new family. They all are usually included in the wedding procession and therefore will be present at the *morning of* as well. Don't call an older teen a Jr. Bridesmaid as this term is condescending to her. Younger teens love it because they are not being considered a *flower girl!* But many times the bride tends to forget how stressful and unsure of themselves younger or older teenager girls can be and may get more than they bargained for by including them in the *morning of* preparation room. Consider a grandmother or an aunt to take over this job in another room. You will have a life together, but you don't have to get ready together.

- **Let the stylist know the ages of any of the Jr. bridesmaids or younger bridesmaids as they may be able to send over a stylist who does well with this age group.**

It may be wise to allow them to have a friend with them. I know this may seem unconventional, but it could prove to be a mood swing saver!

Flower girls can be adorable or a nightmare. If you think you want to use a young family member to be a part of the wedding, keep your eyes open to their personality traits *before* you ask them. Beware of the sister-in-law or relative who assumes you will ask their kid just because they are the correct age. Consider the *morning of* you wish to experience and if it includes children, fine. If not, have your excuse ready and rehearsed well in advanced.

Let me share what I have come to notice and experience in many families over the years. I am an only daughter, so I have no sisters and hence no *direct* nieces and nephews as such. My husband, on the other hand, has three sisters and it seems that the sisters are more apt to call on each other to help out with each other's kids. Grandparents are also more at ease with their own daughter's children, in the sense that they can speak into their lives more freely. I see this with my friends' children and other relatives as well. But here is where I am going with this! When it comes to flower girls and whose *side* they are from, be prepared for a little competition.

A friend of mine attended a wedding where there were to be two flower girls. One was the groom's sister's child and the other was the bride's sister's child. They were cute little blonds, close in age and even wore the same dress size! They were going to be wearing identical dresses. The mothers decided to get the girls dressed at the church after having stayed the night before at a hotel.

- **When everyone arrived at the church, it was discovered that one of the flower girl's dresses was missing.**

The hotel was 45 minutes away, making it impossible to retrieve the missing dress. However, the bride's sister *insisted* that the dress that *was* present was her daughter's gown, but the groom's sister thought it was *her* daughter's gown. Remember: same dress, same size! The groom's sister swore that she did not forget her daughters dress! Now, to add insult to injury, the groom also had two other sisters who were bridesmaids and did not believe the bride's sister either! The groom's sisters all accused the bride's sister of taking "their" flower girl's dress! It finally came time to get ready, and I'm sure things were running late at this point. The bride's sister put the dress on her daughter and the groom's sisters were bawling. In protest, the groom's sisters *refused* to do their hair and make-up and walked down the aisle without "their flower girl"! Red eyed and miserable with no hair or make-up done, down the aisle they pouted! It was so horrible and their behavior so rude that the bride did not want any of her wedding photos from her photographer!

That night, as everyone retreated back to the hotel, there it was: the flower girl's dress was hanging on the door right where the groom's sister had left it!

What a wedding! In defense of the groom's sister (*if I can dig deep for some),* when a family is involved with a wedding, most of the packing for *everyone* falls onto the mother. She has to pack herself, maybe her husband, and most certainly the flower girl and any other children. On top of all the packing, there is the additional worry that the child may not perform her duties well and make mom look bad! If you ask a family member and her children to be in your wedding, make sure she has additional help.

Men:

Why is it when men are around other men they seem to regress back into adolescence? I don't have the answer, but I can prepare you for this transition as it relates to your wedding morning, especially at hotels or resorts. Depending on the amount of time the men have in the morning, and believe me they will wait until the last possible moment to get dressed, they may take off for activities. Sailing, golf or gambling are some of the options I have witnessed the men get involved in. Every once in a while I am surprised by a guy or two who enjoys hanging out with the women in the morning, but they usually want the TV on, and this does not go over well with the ladies.

- **When the men get together, their Neanderthal blood rises and the competition thing sets in.**

The golf game becomes a betting pool. The football game gets too rough. The casino calls out for a third hand and there is always "a good time Charlie" kind of guy who hates to drink alone.

If your nine-to-five groom has not set foot in a boat or on the golf course yet this season, he may not be prepared for the sun, fun and sore muscles that are sure to follow! Gently remind him that you two did not go through all this trouble of putting a perfect wedding together for him to suffer through his vows with sun stroke.

Allow me to share one of my big pet peeves. If your man is in desperate need of a hair cut, hopefully he will not wait until the day before the wedding or the *morning of* to get one! Make sure he gets one at least a week ahead of time! I have seen my share of grooms who get a hair cut that morning or a day to two before the wedding.

They look so handsome all dressed up except for the fact that they have white walls above their ears and around their neck because of tan lines! If it is not tan season and he insists on getting a fresh hair cut, remind him to ask for a shampoo *after* the cut, to remove those clingy tiny little hairs that show up resting in ears and on shirt collars!

Dads are fun to watch on the wedding *morning of.* Some are the jokester type who come into the room and ask, "What can you do with me?" while rubbing a bald head! Some are quiet and nervous and some become emotional.

- **Weddings always spark latent emotions, good or bad.**

Just expect some to come to the surface and you will be prepared and ready to handle them.

Final reminders: for hotel and resort morning of locations:

- You may have unexpected visitors stop by your room.

- Secure the largest room you can afford.

- Tell the front desk not to give out your room number if you don't want interruptions.

- The cleaning crew always knocks to come in.

- Emotional feelings may overflow.

- Children love to run around and explore.

- Cartoons usually win out if there is a flower girl getting ready in your room.

- Rooms may be too small.

- Don't wait until the last minute to order food; plan ahead.

- Have a trial run of your beauty services.

- Make sure vendors have directions and phone numbers.

- Pack a little each day and keep the items in view.

- Visit the wedding site the same season as the wedding, if possible.

- Your resort may be crowded as some resorts are also time-shares.

- Off-season can be less expensive and less crowded.

- Groomsmen may get sunburned playing golf.

- People may drink more knowing they don't have to drive.

- General elevated stress will occur.

Chapter 2

The Morning Of: The Brides Home

For many of today's independent brides, or those couples living together, getting ready at your own home would be a logical choice. If this is your first wedding, it is important to know what to expect. If it is not your first, I guarantee it will be different. To make the most of your *morning of* it is equally important to have a fresh view and to be prepared.

Getting ready at your home seems to make perfect sense. Everything is available so there is no need for packing or extra planning. However, don't become *too* laid back, because *all questions* will be directed *your way!*

- **Every question will come back to you, so it is important to have a plan.**

Guests, who are not able to attend, may call that morning to wish you their blessings. This happens more at home weddings. It is hard to get ready with a phone on your ear! It may be wise to designate someone to answer the phone.

For some cultures, staying with relatives is expected, and family members may end up getting ready at *your* home. If your space or patience is limited, and you can afford it, send them to a hotel or a nearby Inn. You may wish to include a list of local hotels, Bed & Breakfast's and sightseeing spots with your invitations to inspire ideas.

For guests who are financially strapped, it may be worth the expense to book them at the local hotel/motel. Sometimes peace of mind is priceless.

• Think outside the box

As wedding planning begins, many relatives ask how they can help or what you would like for a gift. Your favorite uncle may be glad to cover the room cost for your bridesmaids as his gift to you. A close friend may be willing to put up some of your guests at her home. Ask and you shall receive. Remember you have all day to see everyone. Close friends may try to set up time to visit because they traveled so far to see you, but this is your wedding and they came to see and witness the event. Don't spread yourself too thin trying to have everyone over for a brunch so that you can spend time together. You will need your *morning of* time to relax and prepare for your day.

Be sure to keep communication open with your groom regarding the *morning of* plan. His college buddy may drop a hint that the local hotel is expensive and your fiancé blurts out, "Hey man, don't get a hotel; crash with us-the couch is free" without knowing or even *thinking* that six of your bridesmaids will need that family room in the morning to get ready in!

Where will you sleep?

This one is pretty easy to figure out. But if you are living with your future husband, you may both decide he should find a place to stay the night before. If he is not crazy about the idea, at least arrange for him to pack up and leave early so you can get ready. Make it clear what the *morning of* will look like and he may decide to go out on his own! One of my brides told me she and her fiancé decided to separate for one week up until the wedding day. It was his idea!

Other couples wake up together but then separate to get ready. Some hold to the tradition of not speaking to each other the wedding morning. Whatever you want to do will be the best for your situation. Just think it through, communicate and don't assume he knows he has to pack up and leave.

If guests, bridesmaids or relatives are staying over, think through and plan the shower situation. If any of the guests have small children or you have children of your own, schedule them to bathe the night before. Lay out as much as you can for your guests the evening before. Have towels set out and make everything "help yourself" so that you don't have to run around being a hostess your wedding morning.

- **If you have teens, you may wish to farm them out to friends whom you trust to get them to the church on time.**

Give yourself plenty of time to get ready. Though sleep may seem precious, getting up early will help keep your mind clear.

Make this day special for yourself.

When the stylist comes to you:

This is the one splurge you should seriously consider if you are getting ready at your home. (Here is another *out of the box idea* for someone to give you as a gift: *beauty services*!) The last thing you want to do is send out-of-town bridesmaids into the Saturday morning rush!

If you have a small space, think creatively by making zones: one for hair, one for make-up and one for eating. One bride transformed her tiny New York City apartment office space and created a private zone for me to work. I had a great old wooden desk to spread out my items and a comfortable office chair for her friends. Another bride set me up in her bedroom, which became a quiet private space, keeping the rest of the condo open for guests and her children to roam freely and not hover over her.

Another bride had me at her kitchen table, which was great because of its center location. She was able to answer questions and direct traffic quite well from this space.

- **You need to decide what is best for you.**

Having beauty services in an open space such as a dinning room or family room can be great fun for all, but if you prefer a quiet moment then opt for a guestroom or bedroom. Figure out how many will need services and arrange your space accordingly.

Make sure your stylist knows all the details of how many are having services and what your timeline needs to look like. Together you should both be comfortable with a relaxing schedule.

Has the stylist who is coming to you been to your home before?

Make sure you are both clear about directions and fill her in with any details that may not come up on a map search. If your location is a tourist area and summer around your home means crowds, traffic and craft fairs, check the town's activities on your wedding date and let your stylist know. One bride I was traveling to did not mention it was a big weekend craft event and it took me 20 minutes just to get through the center of town. I heard of another stylist who was stuck behind a parade yet did not know any other way to go.

Traveling out to the salon:

Maybe you did not even give going to a salon a second thought. You *love* your stylist and you loved your trial design, so it is off to the salon for you! Are you a working girl and normally goes to the salon for evening or lunch appointments? Saturdays at the salon are very busy and you may be quite surprised by how crowded it is.

- **Plan your time line around the time you want to be back at home to get dressed.**

If you need to be home at 1p.m. to dress, add up the stylist's time to work on you, travel time home from the salon plus traffic time, if necessary. So an hour for your hair, plus travel time of 45 minutes, may result in a salon appointment time of 10:30. *This is for one person.* If you have three or more girls, then make sure to get more stylists booked so you don't spend the whole day in the salon with one stylist. It is more fun if you all get done together.

If your timeline and number of services requires the stylist to come in before hours, then make sure to get this booked well ahead of time. In October, your stylist may agree to do your hair for your wedding date of August 9ᵗʰ but come a social summer schedule, she may wish she did not say yes or she may forget if the salon's appointment book does not go out a year in advance. Be sure to double-check a few months before.

- **Ask for everything in writing.**

You may also ask to leave a deposit for your wedding morning services and make sure to get a receipt to be fully covered. Some salons do this and some do not. I think this is a great idea either way.

Sometimes I service just the bride at home and she sends her maids off to the salon. Just make sure whoever is driving knows the area and that cell phones and phone numbers are passed out.

Also, prepare yourself that one or two bridesmaids may not like their hair styles and walk through the door complaining. Usually this is a combination of both the stylist's and the bridesmaid's personalities and communication styles not clicking. She may not say much in the salon, but once back home with her gal pals she will let everyone know! Let her figure it out. Someone may help her or your stylist may have a quick fix. But try not to let this get you down.

Into the dress:

Even though it is your own home and you know where everything is, I suggest that you make yourself an area to get ready with everything you need in one place.

- **This is a special day and to make it even more so, create an environment in which to enjoy the process.**

Hang up your gown, maybe off a secure chandelier or on a high doorframe. Put out your headpiece and hang up your veil nearby. Lay out your perfume, jewelry and make-up if you are going to be applying it yourself. Put your undergarments, hose and shoes together as well. Do this a few days prior to the wedding morning. It makes for a beautiful anticipation to a lovely, special day!

One bride and groom had a huge house, and they were hosting their wedding at home. The bride had two pre-teen sons. Fortunately they had a wedding planner take care of everything! I never even saw the kids until it was time to leave. My make-up artist and I were set up in their spacious master bathroom. The bride had everything she needed at her fingertips. We finished with the wedding party and the bride and groom kicked everyone out and decided to get dressed together. The high emotions of the day led to some private time between the two! I just hoped she was not going to mess up her hair! We waited in the kitchen, as I still had to attach her headpiece!

Just because it is your house, don't think you can do it *all* alone! Make sure at least one other person is there to help you dress and share your morning with you. Preferably not the groom!

Food at home:

Since the wedding morning is at your home, feeding your *morning of* guests also falls onto your shoulders. Think through the food situation. Who will be eating? How many? Have it catered if you need to. Have it delivered if you can.

- **Put someone who wants to help in charge of this aspect of the day.**

Get a head count, along with some suggestions and a timeline to this person, and check this off your to-do list! Maybe an extra key to your house would help too!

One lovely bride of mine had just moved into her Manhattan apartment two days before her wedding morning! She graciously accommodated five bridesmaids, her mother, the make-up artist and me. Scattered throughout the apartment were still unpacked boxes! But this bride was *prepared* which in turn kept her calm and relaxed! When I arrived, she had a spot set up for me in a small side room. The bride had even thought to rent a bar table and stool for the makeup artist, which was set up in a bright section of the living room. The dining area table was set up with a lovely spread. She had ordered in a fruit tray with muffins, put out a dish of mixed nuts, and two pitchers, one filled with water and the other one juice. Coffee was set up in the galley kitchen. It was simple and elegant.

Many times I see a little of *everything* being put out as if trying to make sure everyone will be happy with the selections. Don't go there! Keep it simple, especially if it is at your home. You have enough to do!

Another at home bride who was living with the groom also had his best man staying over. She did not think ahead for his morning meal needs. Here he was, standing at an open refrigerator, while I was trying to do her hair and make-up. She felt bad because all she had to offer was some crackers and cheese. You don't want to have to feel obligated to fix food or pop up to make something. I know it may be hard to think about others' needs on your wedding day, but try to plan ahead for this.

Because it is your home, your thoughts will probably be on having as little food as possible, because you may be leaving for a week or two on your honeymoon. But guests, friends and the stylist will need something to eat.

Very large wedding parties may need two meals, so be prepared. Again, *out of the box thinking* will help here too! Why not put Aunt Mary in charge of the morning meal, impressing everyone with her homemade jam and fresh muffins! Or put a groomsman in charge of bringing in a big box of Joe and a selection of bagels and muffins. Order out for lunch or make a sandwich tray the night before.

- **Try this! Ask someone to be in charge of clean up.**

Put out the baggies or plastic wrap to avoid more questions. You will probably be in the middle of hair and make-up and this will be a great help.

Kids at home:

- **They act up more at home!**

Kids, teens and siblings will act up more at home; especially if you are busy and they know you can't pop up to referee! It happens, so plan to make your *morning of* as stress free as possible.

Many of the weddings that I do at the bride's home involve children from a previous relationship. It may be important to the bride that the children are involved. The bride may be trying very hard to include the children and not get the cooperation *she* may need. Many times the children are simply too young to handle the stress of the day. Or they may be teens who roll their eyes at every suggestion and it is not worth the fight. Stop and ask yourself these questions:

- Am I trying to orchestrate and involve the kids/teens because it is what I want?

- Are the children of an age that they can handle and behave in an appropriate manner?

- Are my decisions and expectations being fueled by others expectations and pressures or my need to do it "right"?

Some tough questions, I know, but it is necessary to face these emotions ahead of time.

Another second time bride was getting ready at her home and this time I was set up in the dining room. She had two teenage sons, each used to their own schedules and routine. I don't know what happened, or what was even said, because they were arguing in Russian! Body language, tone of voice and the decibels that were reached told me things were stressful!

A bride's wedding morning, no matter what your age, needs to be as relaxing as possible. Have a talk about the *morning of* well before the wedding with whoever will be present or involved. Ask them to tell you what they are expecting or how they think the morning may play out. They may have no clue. Establish general wakeup and shower times, tell them, or better yet write out what time they need to be dressed and ready so they know. You may need the shower when *they* were expecting to use it. Their morning trip to the gym may have to be forgone, and it would be best if they know this ahead of time. Communication and planning will prevent rushing, blaming and irritability the *morning of* your wedding. Wedding day jitters are no respecter of roles; everyone feels them, especially young people!

- **Try to be truthful and rational with yourself. Planning a wedding is a high stress and emotional event.**

If the best thing for all involved is to have someone else take care of the kids/children/teens, then so be it. If at all possible, have the kids sleep over someone else's house. They can be brought to the wedding dressed, ready and actually excited to see you.

Think about it. What is a normal morning like? Getting the kids ready for school or daycare is difficult enough as you are getting ready for work. Don't try to do it alone if the kids will be with you the *morning of*. Plan ahead to have additional help lined up.

Make it fun for them.

What I said before about teens is the same for smaller children.

- **They don't care if it is your wedding day.**

They do not understand! They even create problems so as to get your attention! I have seen it! Plus they don't like some stranger (me) working on their mother, keeping her from meeting their dire needs!

I did a trial run at a bride's home. She had two grammar school age boys. One I never saw. He stayed in his room playing his video games. The younger one, however, kept popping into his mother's bedroom asking her things or complaining, trying to drag her away from me. He even reminded her, that later that day he had a birthday party to go to so she better hurry and get finished. To get him more comfortable with me, I let him look at my tools and talked with him about doing his hair come the wedding day. As I watched all this, and knowing the wedding day would be worse, I asked the bride if she had anyone to help with the boys on the wedding morning.

- **She had not given it any thought!**

I told her she needed to secure someone to help the boys get dressed and to keep them entertained, so we could get her ready without too many interruptions. She took my advice and come the wedding day everything worked out fine.

Little girls are not any easier. One bride had three adorable daughters. One was in a walker, one was running a fever and the other was running the show! The bride did her best to make everything special for the girls. They had matching *everything*, even down to miniature gold locket necklaces that the bride put on the girls that morning.

- **Remember, as the bride, the sentimental things you plan will mean more to you then to small children. Try to keep your expectations on the low end and you won't be disappointed.**

The bride also had beautiful fresh orchid wreaths made up for the girls to wear on their heads. Not only are orchids very expensive, they are very fragile! The girls kept touching the wreaths and whacking off the flowers. I just kept picking up the flowers and pinning them into the hair to salvage them as best I could! We did not even try to put the wreath on the baby. I told the bride to have someone plop it on her head just before the picture was shot.

- **Just as services were winding down and things began to settle the bride's sister showed up with her kids!**

Think through the day as best you can and think about the children. My eldest daughter was a very active ADHD child and the perfect flower girl age for a number of family weddings that took place when she was young. I would not allow anyone to even think about asking her to be a flower girl. I could not put myself through that! If you decide to involve your children, you may consider choosing a small ceremony with family and friends that is not too overwhelming and then enjoy an adult only reception later in the day.

Another bride that I did at her home had just had a baby and I had to stop doing her hair to allow her to nurse! The groom was there as well as an older son. Diaper bags were packed along with toys for her son, their meals and the veil! She also had an elderly mother who needed her help getting ready. Running late, they all rushed off and left me to see my way out! I had to making sure to go through one of the doors that would lock behind me. I was paranoid about forgetting something inside as I lived the next state over!

Men:

Hopefully your groom found a place to get ready himself. It may be a good idea to talk to the best man yourself to make sure things are in place.

At too many weddings, I have had to put on the boutonnieres for the men. Ask the florist about when and how they will get their boutonnières and if she or an assistant will help put them on.

- **A general conversation about his morning of should take place.**

This should be a conversation, not an inquisition. If you hear bits about a golf game in the a.m. hours and you fear there is little time for this, find out how they plan on working it in. Remind him about sun protection, because sun burns and photos do not go well together.

In general, men don't know what to do with themselves on a day that is not normal. They tend to operate on auto pilot and if their routine is interrupted, they don't make very smart off-the-cuff decisions. You may be a wreck and he decides to wash the truck. For a guy, washing his truck is the same as you going shopping; the truck may not be dirty and you may not need clothes, but both activities serve their purpose.

If his pre-wedding to-do list included fixing up the yard, he may think saving the lawn cutting for the *morning of* is a good idea. Make sure you talk about things like this ahead of time. This may be one morning you will want him to sit and watch a ball game to keep him in a safe distance, clean and relaxed, as long as his team is winning!

Family pets:

Many single women like to have a dog for protection. When a day is not "normal" animals sense stress, especially big dogs.

- **Getting ready at the bride's home takes some planning for your pets too!**

Many times I see signs of a dog and am told that the dog is at the kennel. This is a good call for sure, but not all people can bring themselves to do this. For some, the animal is practically family and they want the dog to take part in the wedding!

When I do trial runs on brides in my home, I put my dog away upstairs before hand. If you are not used to anyone but close friends and family visiting, then it may not occur to you to have your dog put away on your wedding morning! Remember, on any given *normal* day you can jump up and put the dog away when the doorbell rings. But not if you have a hot curling iron wrapped in your hair!

One bride had a huge male German Shepard who, I was told, did not like men. I arrived first and he did his sniffing and we quickly became friends. As I had the bride wrapped in a hot curling iron, the doorbell rang. It was the *male* photographer who proceeded to let himself in! He was kind of entering backwards as he was loaded down with cases, bags and cameras. Well the dog bound for the door, barking and causing quite a stir! The photographer quickly got back outside and waited for the dog to be put away. The poor bride was upset and started to sweat. Her only air conditioner was in her bedroom! With all the commotion, it took some effort to get the dog settled down and put in the basement. Then he spent the rest of the morning barking!

Cats can also disrupt a wedding morning at home. They either totally disappear or act up even worse. Plan for your pets at your home wedding, as animal hair becomes air born with static and others may have allergies.

You *can* have a dog-friendly wedding day! If you have friendly dogs! At one *morning of* the brides two large dogs, well trained and dressed for the wedding in floral wreaths made for a lovely addition to this home wedding ceremony!

- **Your morning of will come with its own inevitable stress but flexible planning, prior communication and proper attitude will help to keep it under control!**

Final reminders: for getting ready at home

- Hire someone to watch and help with the kids.

- Make a list as guests begin to say they are coming and find out where they will be staying if it involves your home.

- Ask special relatives to cover hotel room costs.

- Ask close non-wedding party friends to host guests or children.

- Communicate with your future husband about his morning of timeline and plans.

- Plan enough time for interruptions.

- Hire a wedding coordinator.

- Plan on someone to help serve food and clean up.

- Emotional feelings will overflow.

- Children, any age, don't understand and get stressed.

- Pets need a plan too!

Chapter 3

The morning of: Your childhood home

Whether you still live at home or are traveling back to your childhood home for your wedding, let's talk about the *morning of.* If you still live at home more than likely there is a routine everyone is used to.

- **Be it a work day or a weekend, routines can become pretty ingrained in those who live together and your wedding morning is bound to shake things up, a lot.**

Will you be returning to your childhood home for your wedding? If it has been a long time since you were home, expect things to be quite different from the last time you were there.

Sleeping in your old bed or taking a bubble bath while your mom brings up your toast and coffee may be some of the images floating through your *wedding bliss filter* (each bride inherits this filter the day the ring goes on her finger)…But the actual events that do transpire may not be in agreement with your mind.

- **Memories are strong reminders that elicit genuine feelings. Your mind's eye romanticizes how you envision your wedding morning.**

This is the point where disappointments and stresses can occur. Expectations without detailed planning could spell disappointment. Though such detailed planning may seem to take all the fun and romance out of the day, believe me: best-laid plans are best laid plans! And even with planning, prepare your mind to accept *your* best wedding day and you will recall the great moments for a lifetime!

Where will you sleep?

One bride who was getting ready at her childhood home spent the night in her old bedroom. But *her* old room was now her brother's room. (I think he got a couch somewhere.) Having spent the night in her old room, she assumed she was getting ready there as well. So upon my arrival she led me upstairs and I set up my tools in "her" room. The first thing I look for is an outlet and a place to spread out my vast array of curling irons, pins and sprays. Everything was set up, heated up and I was just waiting for the bride to come back. Well her brother came in and my presence surprised him. He turned on his heal out of the room in a huff. He was not at all happy. This young man wanted "his" space because he needed to change too! So we moved all of my stuff into her parent's room. Time is, well…time. And on the *morning of,* time is precious. Now dad needed a new place to get dressed, so he dragged his tux into the son's room, then he came back in for his socks, then for his belt… well you get the idea.

Another bride who was still living at home, did not allow any childhood fantasy about her wedding to overrule sound judgment. Knowing her home would be overrun with family and guests, she knew it would be better if she got ready elsewhere. She decided the pastor's home near the church was the best choice. Her wedding morning was a lovely and relaxed affair. The Pastor's wife having hosted many brides, was a seasoned professional regarding the *morning of.* She had the living room emptied of extra furniture, long mirrors were brought in and a power bar was ready and waiting for me. I worked adjacent to the living room at the dinning room table, allowing me to see everyone who needed my help.

"The meek shall inherit the earth" as well as a relaxed wedding *morning of*!

Showers:

With a house full of visitors, rehearsal dinners and dressing up, everyone wants to look their best. As the bride, you need to plan your morning first and then have the others work their bathroom time around you. (Yeah right, in a perfect world!) Get a head count of how many will be staying over.

- **Plan for who will need a shower and at what time.**

If your bridesmaids are getting dressed at your home, remind them to come showered, shaved and with their nail polish done the day before. One or more bridesmaids might be a dear friend and remember good times of sleepovers and such. This could lead them to assuming they can shower at their "home" away from home. Showers should be for overnight guests only.

- If there is a house full of bridesmaids or relatives who do need showers, tell them or post a cute sign saying that the bathroom is for "showers only". Then set up a spot other than the bathroom, either in a hallway or spare bedroom where blow-drying and make-up application can take place.

This planning tip keeps the bathroom free for showering and the men that need a sink.

In another home we were set up in the kitchen. The food was spread out in the dining room and this kitchen space was bright and cozy, picnic table style. The space looked out onto the family room where we could see everyone. *These wedding mornings can be great fun!* Laughter and lively talk ensues as old stories are retold. The morning becomes an assembly line of curlers and make-up brushes as the girls work through their beauty services.

My make-up artist and I had just finished with one of the bridesmaids. She looked in the mirror and exclaimed her admiration. She then stood up and announced she was going upstairs to shave her legs! Wait a minute! Now I'm thinking steam does not mix with a new updo or fresh make-up. Why didn't she do this the night before or at her own home that morning? The next thing I knew she was back in the kitchen with a wet updo and runny make-up! She was unfamiliar with the shower, and the last person left the pull up. So when she turned on the water, it poured out of the showerhead soaking her! She had to be dried off, calmed down and redone. This created undo stress and ran everyone behind.

Remember your wedding may be "a first" for many involved!

When a stylist comes to you at home:

Even if I tell the bride that I need a place to set up and work since I am coming to service her at her home, sometimes this information does not get to the mom. Or maybe the bride just assumes things will just work out once I get there. I am not sure where signals get crossed or balls get dropped, but random thoughts of "it will work out" is not a solid thing to bet on the *morning of.* When a bride is still living at home and the wedding is there, an assumption of "mom's in charge" hangs in the air. This all becomes too much pressure on the mom, so it is important for the bride to step up.

I always ask for a large table and a well lit space like a dining room. Even a foldout table in the living room or family room is sufficient, as many of these rooms include a large picture window which helps with lighting. But this next mother had other plans for me. I was welcomed in the home and walked past a perfectly empty table and whisked upstairs to her master bedroom. I have learned that certain cultures are very strict concerning cleanliness, hair and food, so no dinning room table for me this time.

The house faced a busy street as did the master bedroom on the second floor. To ward off the street lights and neighbors, the windows had heavy dark draperies over a sheer inner curtain and the room had no overhead lighting. The spare bedroom would have been fine as it was brighter, but the mother thought I needed a mirror. So she put a chair in front of her dresser, which left everyone's knees hitting the draws and provided barely a view of the top of the head! Not only was this setup horrible, but the dresser was next to the master bathroom and the chair blocked the entrance. I had to move out of the way every time someone went in, not to mention the wave of steam coming out every time the door was opened. I asked the bride if we could move downstairs but the answer was no. Eventually I moved the chair into the middle of the room using a bed to hold my supplies.

As the morning progressed, dad came upstairs to get ready and he did not know we were set up in his room! He was none too pleased and he let his wife know it in their native tongue of Italian, full gestures included.

- **When planning a space for the bride to get ready in the home, make sure to plan around the people still living there.**

Even if a stylist is not brought in for services, the bridesmaids and bride need extra space and plenty of time to get ready.

Traveling out to a salon and coming back home to dress:

Make sure to ask yourself a few questions before you plan your *morning of* salon trip.

- **Who is going to the salon?**

- **For how many do you have appointments?**

Some salons charge a minimum somewhat like a nonrefundable deposit for all appointments ahead of time, just incase someone decides not to show up. Time is money, and wedding parties have a reputation in the salon industry for what we call, no-shows. Many times, not every bridesmaid or mother shows up for services. Mom may feel too stressed and decide not to go, or one of your maids may chicken out last minute and stay behind to do her own hair. I have seen angry stylists on a busy Saturday morning stewing over wasted time and lost income. Most salons pay their stylists a percentage of service income. That means no work, no pay, as very few salons have their stylists on a salary. Ask the salon's policy about wedding party appointments ahead of time.

- **Who is driving?**

- **What car will be used?**

I know this sounds trite, but I have seen someone about to go out for something and their car was taken by someone else for another errand. Remember everyone living at your childhood home is used to having their life and schedule as their own. A wedding changes things, and you may find your little sister is not willing to give up her Saturday morning workout for a wedding! So that means her car is gone too. She knows she has to meet you at the salon at 10a.m. but does not even think about anyone else needing a ride!

One poor bride shared with me her in-salon wedding morning horror. Because of the no-shows associated with wedding parties, some salons and stylists may treat the bride like she is any other client and if this means she has to wait, then so be it. But a bride is not like any other client, nor is her wedding day like any other day. Brides should receive their services on time. Well, this bride was made to wait at least an hour for her appointment. Then she felt rushed with her service. Because of the time crunch and stress, the stylist was having a hard time getting it right and had to redo the hairstyle. Heading home and behind schedule she missed lunch. The bride realized how hungry she was and to save time, she decided her only choice was to drive through for fast food or risk passing out at the ceremony.

- **Wedding stress creeps up and when things go wrong it intensifies the situation.**

The poor bride was so anxious that the food did not sit well in her stomach. She was forced to pull her car over onto the side of the road and threw up her lunch out the door!

Make sure you are comfortable with the salon and the stylist doing your hair. The more bridesmaids you have going to the salon, the greater potential for problems. If you want a *morning of* girl bonding in the salon, make sure the salon is large enough and has enough staff available to cover your needs.

Many times I opened up the salon early to accommodate my brides. I have also opened up on a Sunday for many brides. If you run up against a poor attitude, don't push your way through. A salon willing to work with you is your best choice. Wedding hair is a one-time style, do what it takes to make the experience a positive one.

- **A willing salon with a great attitude is your best pick for services.**

That may mean choosing a different salon than one you are used to. Your trial run is not just about your wedding hair, but is also the time to assess the salon's willingness and attitude in working with you and your wedding needs.

To hold up your end of this relationship, please make sure you arrive on time for your salon visit. Try to show up a bit early, get a cup of coffee and lose yourself in a magazine for a few minutes to help calm down any surfacing nerves.

Into the dress:

The moment has come. Your wedding dress is waiting. Having watched so many brides adorn their gowns, I can only say I am a very privileged woman. When that moment arrives, try to make the most of this time.

- **Getting the dress on at home can be very special and surreal as your childhood dreams become a reality.**

If modesty is important, then set up a room just for you and someone to help get your gown on. How many will be getting dressed at your home? A gown, slips, trains and all the stuff of girls' getting ready requires space. Consider a family room for this. At one home wedding, they used their lower level den as a space for everyone to get ready in. Relax and have fun!

Don't worry if stylists and photographers are present, we have seen it all. We are professionals and are very used to the *morning of.* One bride who was very proud of her figure walked around in just her panties! *That* was a tad uncomfortable! On the other end, one bride who did not want *anyone* to see her in her undergarments got so angry because her mom tried to make the photographer go into her room while she was dressing. Mom wanted all aspects of the day photographed! She was paying the photographer by the hour and was determined he was not just going to stand around.

Brides need help getting into the gown! Many times, after hair and make-up are completed, everyone in the wedding party runs off to get dressed and the bride is left to fend for herself!

One poor bride tells this story about her home wedding. The mother of the bride had a number of sisters who also had their daughters as bridesmaids. Her aunts helped attend their daughters. The bride's mother was helping her mother. The poor bride was left on her own! Now at some point in the morning a neighbor, a close "surrogate mother" to the bride, stopped in to visit and saw all that was going on. She whisked the bride back to her house and helped her with her preparations. No one knew she was gone!

Now back at home it was time to get into the limo. The bride's mom called out for her husband. No answer anywhere in the house! Not only did this mom forget to help her daughter, but she neglected her husband as well! Earlier he had gone to the garage to get away from all the commotion and was still under the car!

Getting ready with too much help can be just as stressful! I have even seen it happen where everyone tries to help, piling into the bedroom stressing out the bride! At one home I heard, "Out, everyone out! I just want mom in here!" This outburst could easily have been avoided with a plan for dressing.

- **Put one person is charge of helping the bride dress.**

Mom may or may *not* be the best choice for helping the bride dress. Only you know your comfort level with your mom. At another home wedding I heard a bride shout out "mom"? I knew her mother was busy with *her* mom, so I knocked and offered to help the bride dress.

Whoever helps you dress needs to be able to see and manipulate those tiny hooks and eyes that some may have a hard time seeing. Add a new manicure or fake nails to the mix and the task becomes nearly impossible. A *real* killer to the eyes and fingers are the tiny buttons on many gowns. One gown shop told a bride to allow for 30 minutes just to do all the buttons! Some gowns are so full they stand up on their own and the bride needs someone to hang onto as she steps in. Many times I am underneath the gown, searching for a foot to find clear ground on the carpet. More than once I have been found under billows of tulle and silk buckling a shoe!

Remember shopping for your gown? Your mother and maybe a friend or two, plus the gown salon staff, are all there helping you dress. It is a surreal time to remember; dreams are coming true and maybe a few tears of joy flowed. Fast-forward to the wedding morning and you may find yourself one of a few ways: *Alone, too crowded or rushed!*

- **Choose someone to help you dress who is good under pressure, flexible and can see well and preferably not in the wedding party.**

This can be the most rushed time of the wedding day, so plan ahead for the right person to help. A close friend, a younger cousin, maybe an aunt who can get down on the floor and buckle your shoes if need be, are some good choices!

One wise bride had a close friend, who was simply a reader at the wedding, help her get ready. She even offered up a shoulder massage and a game of cards to distract nerves while I worked on others. Mom and the maid of honor are sometimes too stressed themselves to be of any help!

One New York City bride I serviced hired a fashion stylist just to dress her; but not all of us can afford such luxury so plan ahead.

Flower girls can't wait to get into *their* "wedding gown" and many will insistently bug their mother asking, "Can I put on my dress yet?" I haven't figured out what is best. Should they be allowed to get dressed to stop whining, or should they be made to wait so the dress stays clean and fresh? That's one for mom's patience to figure out. One flower girl was allowed to put on her dress to keep her quiet but it did not work. After she "won" and had the dress on then she kept asking when she could put her floral wreath on. Once that was on it was just a few minutes before she was asking for her flower basket!

Food at home:

There is a funny story from the Bible and it goes like this. There were two sisters in their home entertaining Jesus and his disciples. One sister Mary sat at Christ's feet, listening to him and enjoying her visit. Her sister Martha, on the other hand, ran all over the house preparing food, fussing about and getting stressed out. She even asked Jesus to tell Mary to get up and help her. Why do I tell this story? Because I have seen my share of Martha mom's catering to a house full of guests at a home wedding while the bride becomes frustrated. Is your mom a Martha running about making sure everyone has what they need? Or is she a Mary, one who will order out, plan ahead and enjoy her guests and your day?

Putting out a spread of food takes up a lot of room, time and stress if not planned properly. Some mothers insist on doing it all, either to save some money or just because they want to do it. As mom runs around feeding and entertaining, she will become stressed. I witnessed one bride become upset as her mom was dividing her time elsewhere and not catering to her long-time childhood request of exactly how she wanted her toast!

- **When it comes to putting out a morning or afternoon spread of food get as much ordered in and delivered as you can afford.**

Personally, I feel more time and creativity should go into the display, and this can be done the night before with fancy platters and pretty napkins. Set everything up so it is "help-yourself". While there is nothing wrong with throwing open a couple of boxes of bagels and donuts, just plan ahead who will go out to purchase them. Put one of the bridesmaid's husbands in charge of this task, one who knows the area!

If nothing has been planned, be rest assured that someone will expect coffee. Sometimes dads get involved by taking orders and then travel down to the local coffee shop. It seems like a good idea, at the time, but I have never seen this go smoothly. Inevitably, one of the bridesmaid's cars needs to be moved so he can get out. If he is not used to this task, he will come back stressed because the weekend lines and local traffic can be crazy!

One wedding party was a house full of women. Dad did what dads do best; he left for a drive. The brother stayed out of sight (good man), and the kitchen was full of women. But the mom was so busy feeding everyone and making sure coffee was being poured that she neglected to save enough time for herself to get ready. Though we arrived on time, our seats remained empty as she scurried about. We encouraged her to sit and get started, and we even promised to put the food away for her! When the wedding services were finally finished, everyone rushed out to get to the church for pictures. True to our word, my make-up artist and I stayed, put away all the food and helped clean up.

- **I have never really seen that much food consumed early in the day.**

Some are too nervous to eat and usually so much is left over. Keep it simple.

Emotions at home:

Mom and dad were still living in the bride's childhood home. One could tell it was lovely and her parents were sweet and kind. But unfortunately the bride's younger brother had died in a car accident a couple of years earlier. While I was doing the mother's hair and making my normal chitchat, she started to talk to me about her son. She said she wished he could have been there to witness his sister's wedding. But this conversation drifted into the living room where the father was. It brought with it a flood of emotion for him that was more than he could take. He popped his head into the kitchen and asked his wife to stop talking about it. The bride got upset as well, because she did not want her day overshadowed by this issue. I consoled the mother and we transitioned to another topic.

- **Lost family members will come to mind during these emotional times and being home makes them all the more memorable. Plan for this and the memories can become bitter sweet and not unexpected and uncomfortable.**

Another bride who was still living at home had set me up in her parent's beautiful sitting room off the master suite. It was on the first floor with sweeping glass doors that entered out onto a patio with spectacular garden views. It was a perfect day and the preparations for the outdoor wedding and reception were unfolding. As lovely and spacious as the room was, this was Dad's cozy spot to watch his T.V. With all the bustling going on with florists, caterers and tent people inside and out, he decided to stay put in his spot. A morning of CNN was more than the bride could handle. Unable to take it any more she asked her mom to "get daddy out of here, that news is depressing!"

When the bride and the siblings are at home getting ready, my past experience is that emotions tend to run a bit freer than if they were guests at a hotel. Some younger siblings, especially males, tend to see "the wedding" as an intrusion on their turf. Remember how selfish the teen years can be? All the wedding talk, planning, expense and *stuff* they have to do sometimes hits its limit on the wedding day. Don't take it personally or expect them to "behave". You all know how stressful the holidays can be; don't expect the wedding to be any less stressful. Crying, "It's my wedding! Why can't you be nice!" may fall on deaf ears.

- **Proper mental and emotional planning is just as important as any other planning you do for the wedding.**

Teens' & children's emotions:

This next bride's teenage brother saw his sister's wedding day as any other Saturday. He slept in. *Teenagers will be teenagers.* The bride was getting fretful, as was the mother. I was set up at the kitchen table. Someone was sent upstairs to arouse the sleeping teen. When he did finally come down stairs, he started to fry up bacon and eggs for his breakfast (while in his tux pants and white shirt!) One foot away, the bride cried to her mom about not wanting her "hair to smell like bacon" on her wedding day. Words were exchanged, bacon stopped frying and beauty continued.

Do you have nieces and/or nephews who will be in the wedding and getting ready there as well? If you have not made the call as to whether you want children in the wedding, I have a terrific article that can help you decide on my web site, www.weddinghair.com. If you do know for sure the little ones will be participating, read on. *Remember, your childhood home is grandma's house too!*

- **The kids may be used to having grandma and grandpa as well as the house, at their beckn'call.**

This can be stressful for the little tykes because they do not understand what a wedding is all about. An added stress is when the children's mother is also in the wedding. A wedding day is not a good day to *expect* any miracles from the youngsters. Planning ahead is the best defense. If it is possible, farm out the older siblings to neighbors or relatives. If they can get the kids dressed and to the church on time, go for it!

For younger ones, hire a favorite sitter to help dress and play with the kids so mom and grandma can get ready too.

For this wedding not only was the mother in the wedding, two of her young daughters were also. On top of that she was the matron of honor! While I did the mom's hair, her two young daughters took advantage and ran wild. One little girl was found hiding under a table with a hand full of bobby pins "doing" her own hair (after I had *just* done it). Then she thought it was great fun to go up and down and up and down the stairs while holding up her dress like Cinderella! I was waiting for a tumble and a fat lip for sure! The bride's sister, though, being matron of honor, was of no help to the bride, nor was her mom(grandma), because she had to watch the kids while *their* mother got ready.

- **Sisters as bridesmaids can be a double whammy of emotions.**

At one wedding the sisters were at odds. The younger sister was the bride and the older sister was unmarried and envious, as the gossip flowing that morning implied. She did not stay for her hair and make-up services, but she dropped off her kids who were the ring bearer and flower girl. Grandpa was supposed to be in charge of watching them. As we serviced the bridesmaids at one end of the family room, he sat in his chair reading the paper. He did not seem to notice the older grandson offering horsy rides to his younger sister, and they were already dressed in their tux and flower girl dress! Someone eventually came into the room, broke it up and yelled at grandpa. The sister never came back for her services and the bride was upset, but not surprised.

Men:

Getting ready at home has a masculine side. Men are a rare sight while servicing a bride and her wedding party at a hotel. Home weddings are different in the sense that I see the guys milling around. It is so funny to see someone wander into the kitchen, usually barefoot, looking bewildered and confused, groping at a tie, saying, "Where does this thing go "or" how is this supposed to hook on?" I have certainly pinned on my share of boutonnières and straightened out a number of ties. Speaking of attire, I have witnessed a number of clothing catastrophes.

• **Each guy should check his own suit when he picks it up (while still at the tux place) to make sure everything is there and is the correct size!**

One groom's tux was missing completely, and the store was closed! One groom's sleeves were hanging over his hands and had to be rolled and pinned hidden in the sleeves of the jacket! One groom forgot his shirt and had to borrow his teenage son's! The poor son who was the best man had to wear a white polo shirt under his jacket! Another time, a suit was missing the pants and black jeans were the only substitute for the problem.

For some families, a home wedding indicates that saving money is a goal. This presents many in the home with responsibilities for jobs usually left up to the catering staff at halls and hotels.

For one home wedding I was set up in the kitchen doing the bride's hair. People were in and out of the room all morning. The bride's twenty-something brother was in charge of getting all of the liquor over to the hall where the reception was to take place. The dad was getting stressed as he had not shown up yet, the time to get to the church was drawing near and he also knew the son still had to get dressed! Well, he did finally show up, but not alone! He had a new girlfriend! He chose his sister's wedding morning to bring her home to meet everyone, and he was planning on bringing her to the wedding! Emotions were broiling under the calm surface of trying to be nice to the new girl yet fuming at the son for this blunder. He was quickly pulled aside and chastised. The problem was that he saw nothing wrong with it all!

Family pets:

Our homes are home to our four-legged friends as well as to us. Animals are very keen to our stresses and moods, and when wedding morning activity takes place at home, the family pet(s) may act up.

- **You may consider having the family pets put elsewhere: either at a neighbor's home, in the basement or at the kennel for the day.**

Also, some of the members of the wedding party may be allergic. I have seen this more than once. A bridesmaid's eyes may start to tear and swell as we are trying to do her make-up and she is sneezing every five minutes. The animals also tend to get under foot and may get tangled in wires and step on gowns. Also static and pet hair is not a good mix.

One wedding I did in the bride's childhood home was in a rural area of Connecticut. I drove up to what I thought was a garage attached to the house. I got out of my car and was dragging my bag past the "garage," which turned out to be a barn. A horse popped his head out to greet me, practically knocking me off my feet! I felt like I was on the set of Mr. ED, but most of you probably don't know the show I am referring too! Then I noticed chickens were running around the yard outside and upon entering the house, cats were everywhere. It was a young family and there were also a lot of young sisters and their children. It felt very homey, as everyone was not used to such pampering. It was a treat to transform these ladies!

Another bride returned home to get ready for her *morning of.* It seemed quiet and relaxed. As I dragged my suitcase up the stairs, the house smelled of fresh-from-the-oven blueberry muffins. I set up on the dining room table, which her mom had covered for me. At this particular home it was just the bride, her mom, her sister and her sister's friend. I was anticipating an easy morning, knowing the bride's temperament. But the bride had brought along her cat. I believe her mother was going to cat-sit after the wedding while the bride was on her honeymoon.

- **Animals, even if they know the home, sense the elevated stress in the air.**

As I worked on the bride, the cat kept meowing at me, wondering what in the world I was doing to his beloved master. I love cats so I talked back to him, which in turn made him jump up on the dining room table to get a closer look at me. He knocked over my curling iron and walked through all my stuff. I thought it was cute, but the bride's mother got upset and shooed him down. Throughout the morning the cat also proved to be quite the escape artist. It was pouring rain and three times he tried to sneak out! This got the bride very upset because the cat did not know the area. The first time the sister ran out to get him. His second attempt to make a quick escape was while the florist was trying to carry in the boxes of flowers. He wasn't done yet; he made his third attempt to escape when I was leaving!

Also, as I was putting the bride's veil on, the cat decided to jump up on the netting! Luckily, since I live with three cats, I did not pull away but sunk quickly to my knees as he did this, and fortunately nothing ripped!

At another home wedding, the family dog was relegated to the outdoors. He was quite fine running about as a tent was being decorated and chairs were lining up nicely. Sometimes after I finish servicing the brides, I like to walk around and take in all the views, excitement and beauty of the *morning of* preparations. I strolled outside looking at the coi pond and the beautiful gardens. There was also a bird cage with butterflies inside sitting on a small table. Just beyond that was another small table, and all of a sudden I noticed it held the wedding cake and *the dog* was just about to discover it! I don't think the baker knew that a dog was outside. I had someone guard the cake while I went to tell the mother that she better have the dog put elsewhere!

Enjoy your *morning of* at home. Getting ready in a familiar space can be very nostalgic and make the bride feel very comfortable. But it can also pose some serious stress if it is not thought out thoroughly! To make the most of this morning, remember my suggestions and tips. Be well-planned and prepare for a *morning of* to treasure!

Final reminders: your childhood home

- A proper attitude will smooth over any bump in the road.

- Have a conversation about the morning of, well in advance.

- At home emotions may run on edge; don't be surprised by their eruption.

- Children don't understand what is going on.

- Everyone processes information from their perceptions, so be patient in hearing each other out.

- Teens still living at home may act out.

- When traveling out to the salon, have everything you need for the stylist near the door. (I can't tell you how many times brides forget their veils.)

- Have photos of your trial run; don't rely on the stylist to remember. (One bride was given a different stylist on the wedding day, so her photos proved to be very important.)

- If a stylist and/or make-up artist is coming to service you at home, have a place set up ahead of time.

- Put everything in writing for the salon or stylists traveling, including the timeline, how many services are needed and clear driving directions.

- Provide a properly lit room as well as a nearby power source.

- Figure out who is picking up the tuxes and make sure that they are delivered at the correct location for dressing.

- Have your toiletries all set out in one place.

- Also have towels in each guest's room so no one has to come to you with questions.

- Plan the showers.

- Make sure the vehicle you will be using to drive to the ceremony is clean.

- If you are getting dressed at the church, leave enough time to get there and get ready.

- Don't assume your Maid of Honor will be there for you. Discuss her duties, but at the same time don't overload her.

- Make your wishes clear. Have someone assigned to help you dress and have a room ready for that.

- Make sure whomever you enlist to help you dress, gets ready well before you.

- Flower girls can't contain their excitement, so have them get ready elsewhere if you feel this is a stress you don't want.

- Think outside the box; turn a family room into a dressing suite.

- Animals are keen at sensing stress and may act up.

- Plan for people's needs, coffee, food, chairs.

Chapter 4

Unique Locations:

Many brides' dreams for their wedding, begins with seeking out a unique location that really speaks to their individual style. If you are one of these couples, you hope to make a memorable statement through your wedding location. That statement may require a quaint local spot such as a bed and breakfast in a lovely setting off the beaten path, or it may be best expressed with a barn wedding and a hay ride! For creativity with high style, your location may be a contemporary art gallery or a historical museum.

- **Your morning of will revolve around your venue choice if you are getting married there as well or staying there the night before your wedding day.**

For a few of my brides, it was their childhood vacation home that became their perfect wedding destination.

Oh summer time! Remember those carefree days of your summer vacation? Late nights with friends playing games, chasing fire flies and enjoying s'mores marshmallow treats from the fire pit? A day of swimming coming to an end, as the sting of a sun burn reminds you of your moms warning about reapplying your sun screen?

Memories hold so much power. There is a term used in therapy called "euphoric recall". Our mind likes to recall the good things and the fun times. It is these strong memories that fuel many brides to pick their summer home or childhood vacation spot as a location to have their wedding. If they are adequate in size and amenities, they make for a beautiful setting. If they are not, there are some ways to work around this dilemma with attention to details and planning ahead.

- **In our mind, our childhood home or vacation home is larger than life.**

If it has been a while since you have visited, it would be a good idea to do so before your plans are in writing. Literally, in your memory bank it will appear larger than it might be in person. All the amenities of a normal home may not be in place, and you need fresh grown up eyes to survey these fond surroundings. Tiny bathrooms and kitchens never really stood out as such before. Power availability and rough wooden floors are some things to consider with high heels and flowing gowns. Also accessibility, dirt roads, grassy lawns and ease of finding the location should be well mapped out for the guests.

These unique locations nine times out of ten will require a tent wedding. Everything, I mean everything, even down to salt and pepper shakers and outhouses may need to be rented!

Unique and quaint locations will require more attention to specific details. Some of these locations can prove to be more expensive and possibly more time consuming in the planning. Hiring a professional wedding planner is a must in these situations.

- **The pay off of a fun time, life long memories and beautiful family photos will all be well worth the investment of a unique location.**

A wedding planner experienced in unique locations will be very helpful. But come the wedding morning, they are busy doing what they do best, getting things ready. They will have a lot of vendors to take care of and will be busy making sure all is going well. That means you and your wedding morning is basically left to you to figure out on your own, and in these locations you don't want any surprises.

Traffic trials:

In the summer season theses vacation homes and small inns are teeming with vacationers and your guests may experience congested traffic in town and problems with parking. For one New England coastal town I serviced many brides in, I knew to give myself at least a half hour extra travel time just to get through the downtown area! Make sure to ask the locals if this will be the case. If so, notify your guests in writing in the printed directions.

- **Also check on craft fairs, harvest fairs and any parades that may be scheduled on your wedding day!**

A parade can set the entire morning off because no one is familiar with the side streets! For one wedding, I was stuck for half an hour in traffic because they were having their annual town celebration and craft fair!

Consider the size of your guest list and the space needed for parking cars. One vacation-home wedding hired a valet company to park the cars on their property. Nice touch! When I explained to the valet that I had to leave in a couple of hours and was just doing hair and make-up, he knew he had to put my car where it could be easily accessed.

If you are bringing in a tent, caterers and renting pretty much everything, they will all be arriving in big, heavy trucks that will also need to be hidden from view! Just remind yourself that they do this sort of thing for a living and come the ceremony time everything will be stunning!

Other location options include bed & breakfasts, quaint inns, vacant mansions, museums, restaurants, cruises, and universities. More venues can be found at www.uniquevenues.com in a searchable database using state-by-state and guest-size criteria. If you need to get ready at any of these locations, you need to be prepared for your *morning of* experience so it does not become one you'd soon like to forget!

Where will you sleep?

If everyone is staying close by in a larger hotel, then be sure to read my chapter on hotel mornings for tips about packing etc. If you and some of your bridesmaids are staying on location the night before the wedding, it might be a good idea to visit close to the wedding to get a feel for the space. If it is your summer home, you may have not noticed the lumpy old mattress as a child, and it could need replacing. The sites and sounds will be fun to rediscover as you envision your wedding morning taking shape out by the pool or lake.

With a summer home location, it would be wise to consider what you may need to do to keep the place cool for your wedding *morning of.* While visiting before the wedding, try to look at your surroundings, scoping out any potential problems such as narrow rough wooden doorways, torn window or door screens, lack of adequate AC and necessary power sources. A generator may need to be rented.

One of my brides had her wedding under a lovely white tent on her parent's summer property. The homestead was charming with screen doors creaking and banging every time someone came in, and the galley kitchen was open to the main sitting room providing a view to the festivities taking shape outside. Crooked rock steps led up to the "cabin" and mature landscaping surrounded the lovely country setting. The home itself was rustic with small rooms showing signs of well-worn love.

- **The main problem for this bride became the lack of air-conditioning.**

In the bedroom the air-conditioning was sufficient for sleeping, but the main rooms were hot and stuffy! A unit in a window may be fine for taking the humidity out of the air for a few weeks in the summer but will not provide enough cool air to handle a wedding day with friends and family about. Lounging around in a tank top, sipping ice tea with your hair thrown in a ponytail is much different from gowns, heals and hot rollers.

- **Make-up was near impossible to do as everyone was covered in beads of sweat.**

With relatives and the wedding party coming in and out of the doors, it was impossible for the system to keep up. Tempers rose and patience shortened as the morning went on. To top it off, this bride's style was formal/classic, and she had chosen a gown with sleeves! She and I ended up having to move out of the bright spacious living area into the cooler, darker bedroom to finish working. The hairstyle she had chosen at our trial run in the *air conditioned* salon was a down hairstyle blown out straight. As she was blasted by the hot air from the blow-dryer, she questioned herself that morning, wondering why. Only the most relaxed, carefree bride is able to handle last-minute changes. This bride was not one of them, so I did not offer a change of style nor did she ask. Also, she did not have a planner, so with every question that came her way, the bedroom door kept being opened. Each time it happened, cool air escaped and her stress level rose.

• Think ahead and choose wisely!

In this case she could have allowed the location of her wedding and the country atmosphere to dictate a cooler carefree style. An outdoor setting on a warm summer day would have been lovely with a hairstyle that was more loose and natural.

Wisely, this bride had all of her attendants arrive already dressed and made-up. She hired me for herself, her mother and grandmother.

If you do plan on hosting the wedding and are having guests stay over as well, make sure your septic system can handle the extra water from showers. Not that anyone likes to talk about their septic system, but this is not something to ignore if you are going to have a wedding at a remote or older location. Consider the showers and bathroom needs when deciding who and how many will stay with you at your vacation home or older location wedding.

- **Also don't neglect old wiring or fuse boxes that may blow with blow dryers and hot tools in use!**

Don't expect an older inn or bed & breakfast with one or two bathrooms to be able to handle your reception party's needs. You may be required to rent facilities. But take heart, bathroom rentals have gone high-end and high-tech. I have seen some beautiful ones at recent bridal fairs with sinks that have running water! Check some out for yourself and have the wedding location you have dreamed of!

When the stylist comes to you:

If you decide to hire in hair and make-up professionals at your vacation location, bed & breakfast or remote location, make sure you communicate the timeline clearly and give specific directions. Some remote locations may not have the quality of services or providers that you are used to as far as talent and availability for your desired wedding look. The local talent pools may be sparse, so if your beauty services are high on your priority list, consider this well in advance of choosing your location and adjust your budget to be able to hire in good help.

- **It is very important to have a trial run, if possible!**

If you plan on having your styling team drive in, they may have to arrive the night before, depending on the distance and time services need to start.

One wedding I did with my team was a two-day affair at the mansions in Newport, Road Island. The wedding morning was in an historic, newly remodeled inn while the weddings, yes weddings, were to take place at the mansions. The bride had two weddings planned for the weekend! One was on Saturday, which was a full blown Hindu ceremony complete with custom saris for the bridesmaids and bride. The Sunday wedding was a catholic ceremony representing the bride's family in full New York style. The wedding planner hired a traditional Hindu wedding specialist for Saturday and the bride brought in her personal stylist from New York City for Sunday. Since there were so many attendants in the wedding party, and the local talent was limited, my staff and I were hired by the wedding planner for the bridesmaids and mothers for both days. A few additional local stylists were hired to help as well with hair and nails. Even though it may have seemed a good idea to hire a Hindu stylist to do the bride's hair in a traditional style, neither the bride nor her hair was anything close to that culture!

- **The bride had fine blonde hair and the stylist arrived unprepared and asking us for help!**

Right then I knew there were going to be problems. You don't always get what you pay for. The bride received her services in her own private and spacious room. The "specialist" ran the entire Saturday wedding morning late by almost two hours! The stress in these situations has a rippling effect, infecting everyone else. By the second day, one of the local girls did not show up as she was so intimidated by the number of maids, their requests and the pressures of the day before. Though the inn was exquisite beyond words, the room we had to work in was very small. We had to fit three stylists, one make-up artist and all our clients into a tiny one-bedroom space. Because of the size of the room, the hot tools and the number of girls in the room, the AC could not keep up. Another make-up artist was in another room. The girls had to go between their rooms for dressing and two other rooms to get made up. Time was lost, as once in a while I had to send someone out looking for who was supposed to be getting ready next. Then another guest, who saw us working came in and also asked for services! It was a crazy weekend to say the least.

- **Even if you have an endless budget, do not neglect space planning for the morning of beauty services!**

Don't be a bride that has tunnel vision and only thinks of herself that morning. A comfortable, relaxed and cool wedding party makes for a better start to a long day or weekend! Asking too many bridesmaids is simply asking for too many problems. If you must have it big, rent an adequate preparation space and have the ceremony as late in the day as possible!

Another bride was having her wedding in an old New England barn! The bride worked for Martha Stewart Living in NYC and the wedding was going to be in the Berkshires in New York. It was a three hour drive for me from my home in Connecticut. Now granted I was the one having visions of country splendor. I mean Martha Stewart connections and all! I drove up to the correct address, which was the main home with an elderly couple sitting outside on ratty lawn chairs. It was a bit run down with cats running about and unkempt grounds. I though I was in the wrong place! The couple pointed me to the chalet on the property where the bride was staying with her sister.

The barn, wedding and reception were at another location. As I walked over toward the chalet, I was met by the bride coming back from the swimming pool, but she was dry. The bride was hoping for a morning swim but decided against it as the pool was not as inviting as the brochure had made it look. The 1970s style loft chalet had a very narrow stairway and worn furniture inside. This less appointed space did not seem to upset the bride. It may be a good idea to visit a location yourself or use a reputable wedding planner so you can be sure to have your morning swim!

This bride was a challenge in that she had very thin, fine texture, blonde hair. At the trial run we decided on temporary extensions. If you need extensions, they don't have to be a big investment or in place for weeks. There are temporary solutions for adding hair into an updo. Check out the web or your local beauty supply. I braided a few rows of tiny braids close to her scalp known as "tracks", and then sewed on some real hair to the braids for her updo. I loved her look, and it fit the style of the wedding. She was chic in an understated way with a modern loose hairstyle and a soft, flowing gown. Of course she worked for Martha! The getting ready space, though rundown, was bright and adequate in size. The morning proved to be quiet, simple and relaxed.

Another bride had a small wedding at an old New England bed & breakfast. I believe she was the only guest for that weekend. She was going to wear a simple gown, her mothers 1960's tiara with an Audrey Heparin hairstyle. I arrived early in the morning as the ceremony was late morning. I always travel with a power bar, extension cords and outlet adaptors as some locations have older wiring and not many outlets.

- **I plugged everything in I needed and pop, the circuit breaker went!**

The bride frantically told me the couple that ran the inn was not expected in until later in the morning. While the bride was on the phone, I decided to try another outlet in the bathroom and luckily it was on another circuit. From then on, if I ever worked at an old house of any sorts, I spread out my hot tools all around the room. If your *morning of* plans are to take place in an "old" building, I suggest you do the same!

At another older Inn we kept popping the circuits as well. I had to plug in some of my sets of hot rollers out in the hallway! It was a terribly sweltering summer day and an additional AC was brought in to help, but the added drain on the power caused problems with the blow-dryers and curling irons.

Knowing your getting ready situation ahead of time will help you decide how to have the bridesmaids arrive. Should they do their hair before they come? Will they be doing it there? This means even more hot tools as each girl has her own! This will require more space, more mirrors and more heat! Try to work out these details so your *morning of* is not sporadic, frantic and full of power problems.

Mansions offer exquisite photo opportunities and proved a sense of grandeur for a wedding and reception. An old massive stone mansion on a beautiful estate was the location for another wedding I serviced. The room we were given to get ready in held magnificent windows as long as the wall with a balcony looking out onto the wedding coming together. The grounds were spectacular and we could see the guys and guests strolling through the gardens.

- **But the rooms inside were empty.**

No furniture of any kind was anywhere! Only a few banquet chairs were placed about after I requested some. There was no table to lay out my tools and make-up; I had to use the mantel place and windowsills to hold everything! Coming from the adjoining bathroom was a noisy running toilet. Not quite the mood setting sound for a wedding morning. I could not take the noise or complaints from the bridesmaids any longer. I put down my curling iron and went in. Lifting up the heavy porcelain toilet cover, I secured the rubber thing inside and the noise stopped. I was teased all morning about being a plumber as well as a hairdresser!

- **Your wedding day is not just about the photos!**

Don't pick your location solely on how your pictures will turn out; think of the whole experience. This type of location had no lodging and hence little character beyond massive stone walls and beautiful grounds. It was only a location for receptions and such. Anything you wanted had to be brought in. When your budget is not a restraining order, and you can afford to rent some antiques or enough flowers to fill such a massive space, then go for it. Otherwise these places can be hollow and cold.

One other mansion I worked at provided a more inviting ambiance with a number of antiques placed about. I was told by the bride it also had a room just for getting ready! How nice. The room I was all excited about was the size of a walk-in closet! It was quaint (which is just another word for small so beware) and decorated with built-in seating, chintz fabric skirting, wall paper, mirrors and high ceilings; charming *but no windows.* This meant no natural lighting for make-up applications! Once two chairs were in place for services and the bridesmaids were spread out along the window seating, there was not any space to dress. Since the wedding ceremony was late in the day, the bridesmaids did not arrive in their gowns. Remember that these locations do not have rooms to stay in, which is where attendants normally get dressed. So dressing had to happen on location.

- **These rooms can be lovely; but if your wedding party is large and you absolutely love the location, ask if they can provide another room to set up in and a screen placed in a corner for dressing.**

This dressing room was attached to the ladies bathroom, which you had to walk through to get to it. That was where the girls had to spread out into to get dressed. When people came in to use the bathroom, they walked into bridesmaid central! The poor girls had to lean on walls to hike up their stockings and the modest ones tried their best to get their gowns on in the stalls, fighting their way into their dresses while trying to keep from falling in!

Traveling out to a salon

If a trip to the salon is in order for you and your wedding party, think through the driving situation ahead of time.

- **Because of expenses already incurred with gowns and flights, not everyone will be able to afford to rent a car and will therefore have to carpool with other attendants.**

Your Maid of Honor may be off picking up your mutual friend from the airport and may not be available to put the finishing touches on your favors with you. Or your dad may be on duty to make these trips and you were hoping to have him around in the morning to help drive to the salon.

If you are going *from* the salon onto one of these unique locations, you will need to plan out what you will be taking and pack the car the night before. If others are taking items to the dressing location for you while you make your way to the salon, make it easy for them by having the items labeled and by the door clearly marked. Even if it is your sister or mother, don't assume they will know what you need. Assuming is always wrong in any situation but it is deadly on a wedding morning!

If not all of your bridesmaids are going to the same salon, make sure they know what time they should be back to get dressed and ready as there are usually getting-ready-photos and bridesmaids photos before the ceremony.

- **If the ceremony time is the only number in their head, then they will be late.**

Be specific and clear at to *why* they need to come back at a certain time or they may take it upon themselves to come when *they* think it is sufficient.

Into the dress:

Typically vacation homes are smaller than a real home. Sometimes it is the same with B&Bs or historical inns. With a vacation home location, childhood memories stem from an eleven year old brain and a visit back will quickly readjust your thinking. A small bedroom that barely holds a double bed and a tiny dresser will be filled up by your gown alone, not to mention someone trying to get you into it!

Even some exclusive resort types of inns have been added onto an older original structure. Many times the bridal suite is in the older section because of its charm and visual appeal. However, these rooms are designed for romance and a couple in love, not for a room full of bridesmaids, moms and a couple of flower girls! You may need an additional room for dressing and getting ready in.

Another bride's vacation home was in a tiny beach cottage. She was home for a Jack and Jill barbeque wedding shower, but she lived across the country. She used this trip home to have her trial run, which was a good use of her time and a good dry run for me to judge my driving time. The whole wedding party was there. The house did not even have a kitchen table, but a counter with two bar stools. I worked in a closed in sunroom among the suit cases and wicker furniture. Though it was air-conditioned the windows let in a lot of sun! Thankfully, upon seeing the close quarters, she decided to have me come to the hotel where some of the attendants would be staying the *morning of!* She knew there was no possible way everyone could get ready, dressed and their beauty services done in this small space.

- **Being able to be flexible and realistic is a good antidote, preventing wedding day freak outs!**

A location that is designed to host weddings is somewhat bride-friendly. But the main focus is on the reception, not the *morning of.* Think about this as you decide where you and your wedding party will get ready. I know the thought of driving in your gown is not thrilling and you envisioned all of your best friends with you in the morning getting ready, but think it through!

Food:

At the *morning of* everyone needs to eat! I don't care if you barely fit into your gown. Have something to eat. Stress wrecks havoc on your nervous system, fluid levels and sugars. If you are also having alcohol drinks in the morning, like mimosas, make sure there are absorbing food choices such as bagels or muffins. If your location serves alcohol, they may not be able to do so until after noon. One wedding party at an old inn wanted champagne and a bridesmaid was not to happy about the "only served after 12" rule!

At locations where you are renting space and having the dinner catered, they may not be set up in time to take care of your morning meal needs.

- **Don't assume anything!**

When sitting down with the caterer, you could ask to add a breakfast or lunch tray onto your meal plan and not have to worry. Or you will need to think your timeline through and plan for feeding the morning crowd. If your wedding is late in the afternoon and your day begins early because of the size of your wedding party, you may need to plan ahead for two meals. Keep them simple and fresh, with protein, salty choices and plenty of drinks. Salt calms the stomach. Wedding mornings are nerve racking and eating is a stress-reducing activity. Don't serve anything heavy or greasy as this will upset stomachs.

- **Be aware of fainting!**

Make sure everyone eats, and if someone has fainted before she will be sure to do so again. My husband's sister fainted at two of the family weddings, so when she planned her wedding, she picked the cool fall season! Many of these unique locations either do not have AC or have limited capabilities, so if you have a swooner in your party, keep her cool and fed.

Also, some of these locations are off the beaten path and don't make it easy to send someone out for last minute food. Plan ahead by either delegating someone to pack a picnic brunch and bring it, or call ahead to have an order delivered. You can do almost everything online these days. Order this at least a month in advance, but it would be a good idea to call a couple of the days before and hear a *real* voice that assures you everything is in order and on the schedule, going to the correct location at the correct time.

- **Delegate these small tasks to someone you trust and have them laid out in writing.**

It does not have to look like military drill instructions. A lovely letter will do. Here is an example below:

Dear Aunt Mary,

Thank you so much for offering to feed my wedding party on my wedding morning! Feel free to prepare or order anything you wish. I know you have Uncle Bob's brother visiting so a simple tray of bagels and muffins is fine. There are eight of us plus two flower girls, the two mothers and Grandma Stewart. You are welcome to have your hair done as well. Just let me know by the 9th so I can let my stylist know in advance. We will need to be able to eat around 8:30 as our hair appointments start at 8 and will go until 11:30. Don't worry about the drinks as my wedding planner does a lot of weddings here and managed to get a coffee station included. We are getting ready at The Lake Side Cottage Inn of Bedford and their phone number is 303-xxx-6757. My wedding planner's name is Linda and her cell # is 303-xxx-2303, just in case. Thank you so much for taking this on for me. It is another thing off my list! I am so excited and look forward to "the day"!! If you have any questions please call my cell: 406-xxx-2987.

Thanks again,

Love, Melinda

Any time a location is unique, it really means everything else is going to take extra thought. A vacation spot in September is not the same as in July. Much of the local color and shops may be closed after the summer crowd has departed. Your favorite morning coffee place with those amazing donuts your dad brought home every Saturday may not even be open for business during the season of your wedding.

- **Many of these inns and B&Bs are in historic districts and have zoning laws in place forbidding chain donut/coffee shops to operate nearby.**

Don't assume a Starbucks or Dunkin' Donuts is around the corner. B&Bs in particular only serve breakfast and only up until a certain time. Ask for an exception if needed.

Music:

Music is a nice addition to this morning nosh-beauty ritual and with a unique location there may not be any piped-in sound, TV or radios. There is definitely something to be said about calming the savage beast! Every family has one! At one wedding the bride borrowed an i-pod and had all of her and her friend's favorite music. I have seen bridesmaids trying to find a radio station at an off-the-beaten-path location. Honestly, at one wedding a sister of the bride was running around frantically trying to find some music. The lack of music was stressing her out and all the chatting was not helping either. This makes for a good segue into the emotions section!

Emotions and kids:

If your family vacation spot is on its second or third generation of relatives, your darling little nieces and nephews have squatting rights as well. Your seven-year old niece doesn't understand that her bedroom is also the one *you* use when you are visiting. They certainly are unable to understand or respect the fact you want the door to the room kept shut to keep your gown aired out, wrinkle free and spotless!

A vacation home holds more memories and therefore will elicit more emotions from visiting relatives. Your cousin may have dreamed of having her wedding there, but her parents could not afford it and she may be moping around with a pout you can't quit figure out why. I know bridal tunnel vision is hard to get out of, but try to see through other's eyes so as to keep your own expectations in order.

For the little ones, they are used to running carefree and enjoy bringing in the random bull frog to scare grandma. This may not work quite the same with your roommate from college who grew up in the city!

Teenagers come in a couple of varieties. Some have matured early and actually behave like mini adults, and some may be nothing but a moody, selfish blob of baggy clothes or a cell phone chatty Sally! This is especially so if the location does not have their usual array of electronic gizmos, cell phone service or if they have to share their room with the cousins from the "other" side of the family. Some teens will do fine, but don't be upset if they are *out there* and uncooperative.

- **Some actually thrive on getting people upset, so don't give in and give them a show.**

This is a good time to discuss who to have involved in the wedding, especially if they are teens. Think through the reasoning for including them. If they are to be new step kids, it may be more about how it will look to everyone than how the kids feel. Holding a family meeting to get everyone's opinion will do more for healthy dynamics then having your favorite Bible verse mumbled by your new 14-year old step son, or a moody Jr. Bridesmaid who hates her hair no matter how many times it is redone.

Babies do not usually do well in an unfamiliar environment. New faces, smells and different sounds can make the best child cranky. Your best pal from college may spend more time nursing and less time visiting; an empty breast takes precedence over her time slot for perfect make-up!

Men:

If the wedding location is a family vacation spot, dad may have taken an interest in getting the house spiffed up or the lawn professionally landscaped. Or he may just go fishing!

- **Don't assume men know what to do.**

They only know that they have to get the tux on at some point and will keep asking you what time that is. This question is always followed by the next question, "What time is the wedding?" and then they say, "But I don't need two hours to get my tux on; why so early?" I've heard it at every wedding.

If you can, set up a buddy system if you have a reliable groomsman to enlist to get the guys off the golf course in time. Because mom is usually all consumed with the bride and maybe a grandma or two, the "dad" may get lost without her direction. Remember men like to get the most out of their times and vacations and to them a wedding away is like a vacation. Unfortunately their thought process goes something like this, "If I have to give up a perfectly good spring weekend then at least I have to get in a round or two of golf."

Pets:

I have not seen furry friends an issue at any unique location unless it is a family vacation spot, which always included the family dog. Ask and beg if you must to have the dog put up elsewhere for the wedding day or weekend.

If you *want* your dog to come because you think he will look so cute in a floral wreath and great for pictures, then go for it if you have the needed support of others who will have to take care of the pet. But if you are finding resistance, it will be in your best interest to listen to reason.

If your location has animals of its own, it would be good to know this ahead of time! A barn may mean horses and/or cows and that means hay. Hopefully allergies will not be an issue for anyone that day. A bed & breakfast usually means a private home for the hosts and that may include a dog or cat or two.

There is one unique location I will never forget! This bride and groom had their heart set on getting married on the platform of the Cyclone Rollercoaster in Brooklyn, New York! It was great! After the vows, which took place on the platform of the rollercoaster, the entire wedding party hopped into the cars and went around for two runs! It was a blast to watch this wedding. After a couple of runs around the track we planned on getting together one last time to fix her hair before the reception.

However her reception was to be held at the adjoining aquarium! All morning while getting the wedding party ready, we were serenaded by *seals* barking just around the corner. Her *morning of* getting ready spot was in a big conference room of the aquarium. It was an old converted theater complete with a stage but NO air conditioning! Big floor fans blew over us, keeping us somewhat cool but also making it difficult to keep the hair in place. This was simply the most entertaining wedding I have done to date, so I brought along my husband. We strolled through the old small aquarium and marveled at the setup taking shape for the wedding. Seals may not be pets, but I had to fit this story in somewhere!

I have showed up at way too many wedding mornings where no one had any idea what typically transpires, especially at unique locations! Even if you as the bride have been a bridesmaid countless times, it does not always prepare you for your wedding morning especially at a unique location.

You have spent so much time envisioning your wedding day and by thinking through some of the *morning of* details in this chapter, you will be able to put the brakes on many unforeseen stresses and drama.

Final reminders: Unique locations

- When visiting these locations, picture all of your girls, all their stuff and gowns hanging everywhere. Is there room?

- Check for adequate outlets.

- You may need to get ready somewhere else and drive to these types of locations.

- Don't forget to ask about fairs, parades and detours.

- Air conditioning may not be sufficient.

- Emotional feelings may overflow.

- Will you have to do a lot of "gown lifting" to prevent grass stains?

- General elevated stress will occur.

- Parking may be a problem.

- Will you need to rent décor?

Chapter 5

Destination weddings:

Lisa Light, of Destinationbride.com, has this to say, "You're not just planning a wedding; **you're planning a destination wedding**! Weddings away from home can be exciting, adventurous, and complicated." Lisa is upfront. She knows what hosting a destination wedding involves, and she wants you to know!

Lisa adds, "Planning a wedding far from home can be complicated, and it always takes longer than you would hope for all of the pieces to come together. In the first flush of excitement, couples can make a good start, but they quickly realize that research and follow-up takes time, and little progress is made when they can only steal a few random hours a week for planning. Dreaming is easy. Making your dreams a reality, on the other hand, can seem overwhelming." Lisa has made the process easier for anyone wishing to have the destination wedding of their dreams with her book, <u>Destination Bride: How To Plan A Wedding Anywhere in the World.</u> In her book, Lisa broke the process down, step-by-step, as a roadmap for couples who know they want a destination wedding, but don't know where to begin in planning one.

- **With a destination wedding it is important to put every aspect into perspective.**

Think about what it takes to get ready for a vacation. Then add onto that tons of wedding details and legal stuff you may not even know about. Mix in your best friends and family and you are bound to have a great time. However, understand that you will need the necessary foresight and tools to make it all happen.

Anyone seeking to get your business has to be a salesperson, and this is where things can sound simply tantalizing and romantic. But how do you know which company to trust with your special day? If destination wedding planning is an area you know nothing about, how do you even know what you will need? You may not even have a specific idea of where to go. A good start is to educate yourself. I highly recommend books. (Of course I recommend Lisa's.) Because you need to take in knowledge, and not be swept away by beautiful images that web sites use to lure you in. Books help to eliminate emotions from taking over. You can write in the margins and go back to them often. When spending time researching on line, set up a folder on your desk top, and book-mark sites to come back to later.

- **As with anything you plan concerning your wedding, make sure you do your homework and write down every question you can dream up.**

While searching through service providers, it is always a good rule of thumb to settle on and inquire from at least three companies. This is something I learned from my contacts at, The Association of Bridal Consultants.

- **Whether it is a photographer, florist or any vendor, getting at least three contacts will help you not only to understand what a particular vendor does, but will give you a better sense of who stands out, and who you will feel comfortable with hiring.**

Have you ever seen those design shows where three designers have the same room to design? They are each challenged to put together a detailed plan, hoping to win over the couple. Each designer meets with the couple, but each proposal ends up being uniquely different. The goal for each designer extends beyond simply meeting the couples needs, and reaches deep into an emotional relational partnership between the consumer and the designer. *This connection and understanding, which any wedding vendor should attempt to establish with the couple, is the measuring rod, you, as the bridal consumer, need to hold up against the destination wedding company you choose.*

Be sure to ask for references, and follow through on them. This may be a good task to give to your fiancé. Not only will it get him involved with the decisions, it ultimately involves money. Men tend to enjoy business-like tasks. When it comes to helping out with the wedding plans, men shy away from tasks or decisions requiring "feelings." Checking references is concrete, and the person on the other end of the phone might be more direct and business-like answering questions from a guy.

If at all possible, try to visit your wedding location ahead of time or hire a wedding planner who always visits locations they recommend.

I also spoke to Narelle Williams, of Globalweddings.com. au. The site opens with this, "How about a sunset wedding on a private secluded beach, or an intimate wedding and reception, with your closest family and friends, in an exotic location?" Who could resist! They also say they will fit any budget which is very helpful, (not everyone is looking for 5 star accommodations.) "Getting married overseas, what could be more exciting? Global Weddings can co-ordinate everything from the travel booking for Bride and Groom and all of the guests, to the legal paper work, along with the ceremony and reception. This includes things like flowers, weddings cakes and even photographers. We will do everything for you; this saves you time and stress."

- **Time, stress and budget are key wedding buzz words for sure.**

Now let's address your concerns for your wedding morning at your destination location. Though you will find useful tips in all of the other chapters, I posed a number of questions to both Lisa Light of Destinationbride.com, and Narelle Williams of Globalweddings. com.au.

Both ladies took time from their busy bridal schedules to help me out and I greatly appreciate their knowledge.

1. **Do most destination locations who host weddings offer someone on staff to perform beauty services?**

Lisa offers, "Rarely, although 5-star locations usually have an upscale salon in the hotel".

Narelle tells me these services can be part of a custom package that is prepaid.

2. Do most places offer a list of outside vendors and resources for beauty needs?

Lisa, "Not most, but many hotels and resorts may have a list of recommended salons or stylists."

Narelle: "Some locations do not have much to offer outside of the resort, and it would be best to work with the staff there."

3. What should the bride ask up front about beauty services when planning a destination wedding, any specific concerns?

Lisa, "I highly recommend to destination brides to take a planning trip...honestly it is the only way to ensure a smooth wedding. This way, they can plan on a trial or at least interview stylists and look at their portfolios. If they are eloping or simply cannot take a planning trip, they should get the phone, fax and emails of all of the stylists the location recommends and then try to correspond with each. This way they can determine if they are right for them, find out the costs, and the bride can send photos of the styles she likes, to see if the stylist will be comfortable recreating the design. I also recommend that the bride arrive 3 days in advance in any case and 5-7 days in advance if she did not take a planning trip, so that she can receive a trial run with the stylist. Of course, you will always have some brides, who are just as happy to trust the stylist to make them look nice the day of. Also, make sure when they do have their trial that they take their headpiece or veil along. The brides should be sure they understand the fees involved, and they should find out if the stylist speaks their language. Also make sure the stylist is willing to come to them on the day of the wedding."

Narelle: "For Asian and pacific weddings, our first recommendation to the bride is to do her own make-up or have a friend help out. Most of the brides I work with tend to go for something light and more natural. Many times, the climate prohibits heavy bridal make up. The hairdressers seem to not have any problems with casual updo's adorned with flowers, which suits the hotter climates."

4. What glitches have you seen occur with brides that could have been avoided with better planning concerning hair and make-up?

Lisa, "If the bride is buying a "wedding package" she may find that she has little input and little to no direct contact with the service providers. I am not comfortable with this. There should always be direct contact, because details get lost in translation when the wedding planner is trying to communicate to the stylist what the bride wants. If the service providers do not speak the bride's language....beware....get a translator or take your own stylist if the budget allows. The bride should carry her veil on the plane, along with the gown to be sure it arrives, and the same goes for her special wedding day makeup and jewelry. They should also be sure to get the same stylist that did their trial, or the one who they have communicated with throughout the planning. It is a good idea to write up a simple agreement stating the date, service, stylist, and fees that you understand you are getting, and fax or email it to them to sign. This way they will know you mean business. Brides should also send a picture of themselves to the stylist, so they can give input."

Narelle adds, "You can pre pay all of your beauty services like nails, massages and facials".

While these services don't require any pre-correspondences, you may want to have some conversations or e-mail exchanges regarding hair and make-up, as Lisa suggests above.

5. If doing her own hair, should the bride ask about power adapters etc?

Lisa, "Very important! You can get this information on tourism sites, or the embassy/consulate sites. If you need an adaptor, you can get them at Radio Shack. Many hotels do have hair dryers, but they are not very strong.

Narelle, "Yes, check the voltage and which adapters are correct for the country

6. Do places/locations "run" at a slower pace then in the U.S., and should the bride be mentally prepared for this?

Lisa, "Absolutely. That is why it is important to try to communicate on paper and in person. Also the brides should be warned that prices are not always what they might expect them to be. Some services may be much cheaper than the US, while some may be more expensive than in the US. Italy is a good example. Wedding receptions and photography tend to be less costly than in the US, but the hair and makeup is very pricey.

Narelle, "Absolutely, Destination Weddings are for people who are more relaxed about things and they cannot expect a wedding to run the same as where they are from.

7. Please include anything else you think the bride needs to know concerning her beauty needs.

Lisa, "Keep the climate in mind, especially if the bride is doing her own hair. Does her hair curl in humidity? Will it be hot? Be sure not to sun burn before the wedding day! Also very important....they should be sure they know the tipping customs. This is included in my book as well. They should ask someone whom they should tip, and how much."

8. What time of day do most of the weddings occur?

Lisa, "With our weddings taking place all over the world, and in different venues, times vary."

Narelle: Most of our weddings are from 3pm till 5pm. You don't want to have the ceremony too late, or you will miss having your after wedding ceremony photos taken at sunset."

As I (Gretchen), researched destination wedding web sites, and took some time to view couples wedding photos, I saw the full range of wedding and bridal styles. Some brides and their wedding parties looked just like any wedding I have done in the states, (but with much more exciting photos!)

Many had complete wedding parties, children in the procession, strapless fitted gowns, and formal bouquets; "done" updo's and full make-up. Others, choose a less formal feeling, and went with the beach-y flowing gown, bare feet and loose hair with light make-up.

You need to be honest with yourself about your style, and then suit your arrangements to fit your needs.

Closing comments:

Be sure to read all of my tips concerning the wedding *morning of* in each chapter, as you will be sure to glean many helpful and stress preventing tips, no matter where your wedding *morning of* takes place!

Once your wedding day arrives, know that you have done your best to make your dreams come true. Enter your *morning of* with joy, an open attitude and be determined to have fun! Enter your marriage with everlasting commitment, and endurance.

God Bless You!